UPROAR IN THE HOUSE

Seven Hundred Years of Scandal, Lies and Politics

UPROAR IN THE HOUSE

Seven Hundred Years of Scandal, Lies and Politics

TERRANCE DICKS
Illustrated by Richard Robinson

PICCADILLY PRESS · LONDON

Text copyright © Terrance Dicks, 1993
Illustration copyright © Richard Robinson, 1993

Phototypeset by Spooner Graphics, London NW1
Printed and bound by WBC, Bridgend
for the publishers, Piccadilly Press Ltd.,
5 Castle Road, London NW1 8PR

A catlogue record for this book is available
from the British Library

ISBN 1-85340-230-3 (hardback)
1-85340-235-4 (trade paperback)

Terrance Dicks lives in North London. A very well-known author, he has written over a hundred books for children including the following series for Piccadilly Press: *The Adventure of David & Goliath, Jonathan's Ghost, A Cat Called Max*, and *The MacMagics*. Piccadilly Press also publish his popular information humour books, *Europe United, A Riot of Writers*, and *A Riot of Irish Writers*.

Richard Robinson lives in North London, and is a well-known puppeteer. He was director of the Covent Garden Community Theatre, and has written and developed the Puddle Lane and Riddlers series for ITV. He illustrated Neil Inne's *Gloom, Doom and Very Funny Money* published by Piccadilly Press.

CONTENTS

INTRODUCTION BY LORD WEATHERILL

INTRODUCTION

Parliament has been my life for the past 30 years. It is a continuously fascinating and invigorating experience. Having been a Whip in Government and in Opposition and then Speaker of the House of Commons and now a Cross-Bencher in the House of Lords, I think I can fairly claim expert knowledge of both Houses of Parliament.

There is no shortage of learned books on Parliamentary procedure and many politicians – some famous and others less so – have written about their personal experiences. What I like about this book is that it gives the facts in a light-hearted and accessible manner. It explains the passage of a Bill through both Houses until it receives royal assent (still given in Norman French – "La Reine le veult"!) and becomes an Act of Parliament. It outlines the duties of the Party Whips and what a Three Line Whip actually means. It defines the role and the responsibilities of the Speaker and, incidentally, it clearly demonstrates that behaviour in the House of Commons today is infinitely better than it was in days gone by!

The sprinkling of Richard Robinson's illuminating and amusing cartoons and sketches, plus Terrance Dicks's easy to read style, make this a most enjoyable book to read – I thoroughly recommend it.

The Right Honourable Bernard Weatherill
Speaker of the House of Commons 1983–1992

Part One

Part One

PARLIAMENT IN HISTORY

IN THE BEGINNING

WHO'S IN CHARGE HERE?

As that famous Parliamentarian Winston Churchill once said, *'Jaw-jaw is better than war-war.'*

The dictionary defines Parliament as: *'a formal conference for the discussion of public affairs'*. In other words, Parliament is a place where problems can be resolved by talking, not fighting.

It took quite a while for this idea to catch on. In its earliest form, Parliament arose out of the group of nobles, ministers and courtiers around the king. In time, Parliament developed from the king's cronies and court hangers-on, into an institution with which the nobles, or some of them anyway, could curb the king's power.

At first, Parliament was held wherever the king happened to be. By the end of the fourteenth century it had settled down in the Palace of Westminster, and in the early sixteenth century the Palace's Royal Chapel of St Stephen, no longer used for worship, was handed over to the House of Commons.

DE MONTFORT MAKES A START

Way back in the thirteenth century, Simon de Montfort, a Frenchman who had inherited estates in England, rebelled against the royal authority, defeating both the king, Henry III, and his son Prince Edward in battle.

In 1265, de Montfort called for a 'Great Council' to meet at Westminster, with every shire and town sending two representatives, to discuss England's future. This assembly is often seen as the beginning of England's parliamentary system. It didn't actually achieve much, but it was a start . . .

KING EDWARD CARRIES ON

Some years later Prince Edward staged a comeback. De Montfort was killed – but the idea of having some kind of Parliament lived on. When Edward became king, he revived de Montfort's idea of the Great Council, inviting every country shire and city borough to send two representatives.

PARLIAMENT'S PROGRESS

The parliamentary idea took root in English society, evolving into the system we know today. By the middle of the fourteenth century, Parliament had divided itself in two, hereditary noblemen (and today, life peers) and bishops in the House of Lords, and elected representatives forming the House of Commons.

In the years that followed, sovereign and Parliament struggled constantly for power. Parliament still wasn't a permanent body with regular sittings, as it is now. It met only when the king called it together – and the king only summoned Parliament when he needed more money!

This was Parliament's main advantage. It controlled the money-bags. The most popular royal pastime of the day, invading your neighbours' countries, called for large sums to pay armies and buy weapons. If the king wanted to raise *extra* taxes for a nice little war (not to mention a new palace – or a new mistress), he needed Parliament's consent.

Parliament's influence grew greatly during the reign of Henry VIII, the one with the six wives. When he wasn't getting married Henry was fighting wars, and Parliament got used to being summoned. They started to look upon it as a right ... Not surprisingly, most kings didn't care for this much. Some of them started trying to ignore Parliament, overriding its authority or packing it with their supporters. But it was dangerous to push Parliament too far ...

GUNPOWDER, TREASON AND PLOT

In 1605 a band of Catholic conspirators, led by a certain Guido Fawkes, planned to blow up king, peers and MPs as they gathered for the opening of Parliament. But then, as now, political conspiracies tended to suffer from leaks. The government got wind of the plan, searched the cellars of Westminster, and found them stacked with barrels of gunpowder. The plot was foiled and Fawkes and his fellow-conspirators came to a sticky end on the scaffold. We still remember him with bonfires and fireworks on Guy Fawkes Day, November the fifth. (Disgruntled voters have been heard to say that poor old Guy Fawkes was the only man who ever went to Parliament with a sensible policy.)

PARLIAMENT RULES – OK?

More than most kings, Charles I resented Parliament checking his power – so he dissolved it, refusing to recall it for 11 years.

Led by Oliver Cromwell the Parliamentarians (people in favour of Parliament) revolted and in 1642 the Civil War began. After years of on-and-off struggle, Parliament won. Defeated as he was, Charles I would make no concessions, refusing to promise to summon Parliament regularly in future.

Put on trial, he refused to recognise the authority of the Court. As far as he was concerned, monarchs ruled by 'Divine Right' – their authority, which was given to them by God, couldn't be curbed or questioned. The Parliamentarians didn't agree. In 1649 they settled the argument by beheading him.

For the one and only time in its long history – well, so far anyway – Britain became a republic. Unfortunately, the republic soon became a dictatorship. In 1653 Cromwell was declared Lord Protector, ruling the country till his death in 1658.

THE BUST OF CHARLES I STILL STARES WISTFULLY AT THE PARLIAMENT
THAT DEFEATED HIM, JUST ACROSS THE ROAD FROM THE FAMOUS STATUE
OF HIS NEMESIS, CROMWELL

COMEBACK FOR A KING

By now Britain had had enough of being a republic. The British soon kicked out Richard, Cromwell's son, from his inherited post as Protector. In 1660, Charles II, exiled son of the executed monarch, was invited to return to the throne.

The Parliamentary revolution hadn't lasted all that long, but it had made its point. After poor old Charles I lost his head, future monarchs tended to watch their step . . . .

The restored Charles II had no wish to 'go on his travels' again. Although he had his share of problems with Parliament, he treated it with some caution, doing his best to control it by persuasion, influence and the best method of all – bribery!

CHARLES II WAS INVITED BACK

PARTY TIME

It was during Charles II's time that the party system got going. The king's supporters, the Court party, became known as Tories – an old name for Irish cattle thieves.

Their rivals, drawn from the newly rich and powerful city merchants and from aristocratic families who wanted to check the power of the king, were called Whigs – a term originally applied to murderous Scottish robbers. The party politicians were slanging each other from the start.

It's important to realise that in those days the parties weren't really as firmly grouped as they are today. Throughout the eighteenth and much of the nineteenth century it was hard to tell who was in power – most governments were formed from coalitions of different groups. Alliances were constantly broken and regrouped.

Nor were the parties divided by firmly held political ideas. They were just rival groups, taking it in turn to grab the top jobs, the power and the profits that came with governing the country. (Cynics might say things haven't really changed much . . .)

THE FRONT BENCHES WERE SET TWO SWORD LENGTHS APART,
TO PREVENT FIGHTING

CHECKS AND BALANCES

By now it was clear that the British wouldn't tolerate autocratic
kings any more – but they didn't like repressive republics and
too-powerful Protectors any better. What they wanted was a nice
cosy monarchy, restrained by the House of Lords and the House of
Commons – who also kept a suspicious eye on each other. It was
called a system of checks and balances and it has worked, more or
less, ever since.

THE GLORIOUS REVOLUTION

This system was demonstrated some years later when Charles II
died. He was followed, in 1685, by James II, who was too keenly

Catholic to please the largely-Protestant English.

Far from satisfied with his strongly pro-Catholic policies, Parliament asked William of Orange, Protestant ruler of Holland to take over the job. William landed, James prudently retreated, and the Glorious (because bloodless) Revolution of 1688 went ahead.

In 1689 Parliament met and formally invited William and his wife Mary to reign jointly as King and Queen.

PARLIAMENT STARTED TO CAST AROUND FOR A NEW MONARCH

PARLIAMENT RULES – WELL, SORT OF . . .

Parliament's ultimate control over the monarchy had been confirmed. They'd virtually *appointed* a new king and queen – just like a big corporation choosing a new Chairman of the Board. Being the sovereign was still top job – but it carried obligations and responsibilities, and, as both Charles I and James II had discovered, it wasn't necessarily a job for life. (Buckingham Palace please note!)

The Parliamentary system as we know it today was beginning to take shape, though royal power hadn't entirely disappeared. For a long time the king attended the meetings of his ministers – which must have put quite a crimp on the discussions. In the time of William and Mary the king expected to choose his chief ministers himself. However, things were changing. Queen Anne, who came to the throne in 1702, allowed herself virtually to be ruled by Parliament. The German-born George I who followed her in 1714 *had* to let Parliament rule. He didn't speak any English, so he had very little idea what was going on!

WHAT A ROTTEN LOT!

Although Parliament was getting more powerful, it still wasn't truly democratic. The franchise – the right to vote – was determined by property qualifications. Only about 10 per cent of men – and no women at all – had the vote.

WOMEN DIDN'T HAVE THE VOTE

" SORRY, YOUR MAJESTY –
REGULATIONS IS
REGULATIONS !"

The distribution of seats was all over the place. Little villages of two men and a boy might send a member to Parliament, while some big industrial towns had no representative at all. True, the influence and authority of the House of Commons was growing steadily. But this didn't bother the Lords – they were running the Commons anyway.

MPs weren't paid in those days, so you had to be independently wealthy to take the job. The biggest group of MPs consisted of the sons of peers!

There were numerous 'rotten boroughs', so-called because they could easily be controlled by bribery. There were even 'pocket boroughs', virtually owned by one particular family. With a mixture of threats and bribes, a powerful nobleman could control a block of parliamentary votes – anything from about five to forty-eight. The greater the number of votes, the greater a peer's influence.

HUSTINGS IN A ROTTEN BOROUGH

THE FIRST PRIME MINISTER

Our first proper Prime Minister was a Whig politician called Sir Robert Walpole. He got the job in 1721 and held on to it for 21 years, still a record. (Eat your heart out, Mrs T.)

Walpole entered politics in 1720. He had no problem in getting into Parliament – his family owned a handy pocket borough.

Walpole was a tough, red-faced country squire, described at the time as *a coarse, noisy fellow*. He liked good food, strong drink and dirty jokes, saying that he *talked bawdy because all could join in*. One of his colleagues said of him, *He was of a perfectly even temper and the most good-natured man living.*

Walpole was a famous host as well, entertaining friends and supporters at his country house in Norfolk. One of them, Lord Hervey, said, *We used to sit down to dinner, a little snug party of about thirty-odd, up to the chin in beef, venison, geese, turkeys etc, and generally over the chin in claret, strong beer and punch.*

Despite all this high living, Sir Robert Walpole was a shrewd politician and a master of the dodgy art of high finance.

THE BUBBLE BURSTS

Walpole's big opportunity came in the wake of a financial scandal called the South Sea Bubble. This originally well-intentioned scheme was for the newly-formed South Sea Company to take over part of the national debt in return for a monopoly of trade with South America. Money poured in, share prices rocketed and so did the company's debts which rose rapidly from ten to 40 million pounds. Inevitably the bubble burst, in a welter of scandal. The lucky few who got out in time made fortunes, but thousands were ruined. Accusations of financial corruption implicated a number of ministers, and several of the king's mistresses.

WALPOLE'S PEACE

Walpole was brought in to sort things out. Many of those involved were his opponents, but Walpole decided that the stability of the country was more important than political advantage. He master-minded a massive cover-up, earning himself the affectionately mocking title of *'Lord Screen-All'*. (Big-scale government cover-ups have been a regular feature of political life ever since.)

In 1721, King George I appointed Walpole Chancellor of the Exchequer. Walpole held this and other top jobs, sometimes several at once, for the next 20 years.

By now the inner group of MPs, the ones who held the really top jobs, had become known as the Cabinet. (The name comes from the small private apartment, or 'Cabinet', in which Charles II used to consult his leading ministers.) The leader of the Cabinet became known as the Prime – the first, and most important – Minister.

WALPOLE'S CABINET

Even when George I was succeeded by George II, Walpole managed to stay on top. (There were rumours that he was rather more than just good friends with the new queen.)

Besides balancing, not to say cooking the books, Walpole's main priority was to secure for Britain a period of peace and prosperity. In 1733 he proudly told the queen that 50,000 men had died in Continental wars – *'and not one an Englishman'*.

JENKINS'S WAR

But in those days war was like football, a kind of national sport, and the Brits were getting fed up with the lack of away wins. For some time the Spanish had been stopping British ships suspected of illegal trading with Spanish colonies. They boarded the ship of a certain Captain Jenkins, and in the resulting scuffle, the Captain lost an ear. Recovering the severed appendage, the indignant Jenkins pickled it in a bottle and brought it back to England, where it was displayed in Parliament.

The incident sparked off a storm of patriotic indignation, and by 1739, Walpole was reluctantly forced into war with Spain – a conflict known as 'The War of Jenkins's Ear'.

THIS MUST MEAN WAR!   ...UM - PARDON ?

JENKINS'S EAR

WALPOLE'S DEFEAT

It was the War of the Austrian Succession that brought about Walpole's eventual downfall. George II had joined in to safeguard his Hanoverian homeland, but in 1741 he lost his nerve, signing a treaty with the French before the fighting really got going. In Britain the treaty was seen not as a draw but a defeat, and Walpole got the blame. He still had the full support of the king, and not so long before this would have been enough to keep him in power. But times were changing, and without the backing of Parliament, Walpole couldn't go on. After defeat in the Commons he resigned, going to the House of Lords as Earl of Orford.

A PLACE FOR THE PM

Although his enemies accused him, quite rightly, of filling Government posts with his friends and relations, Walpole was pretty honest for an eighteenth-century politician. He was a master at working the corrupt system of his day, controlling people and events by judicious bribery. *There is enough pasture for all the sheep,* he used to say. He was quite willing to bribe a bishop if necessary. *'Is he mortal?'* he would ask – meaning 'Can this particular bishop be bribed?' (Most of them could.)

Walpole did accept the gift of a house in London – but only in trust for all those Prime Ministers who were to follow him. The address was Number Ten, Downing Street . . .

THERE GOES THE NEIGHBORHOOD!

THE PARLIAMENTARY PITTS

Despite his defeat, Walpole's party, the Whigs, managed to hold on to the Prime Ministership. However, they just couldn't come up with another leader of Walpole's stature. He was followed in the job by a string of well-meaning but incompetent Whig politicians. The next really notable parliamentary figure was a Tory.

William Pitt, known as Pitt the Elder (to distinguish him from his son, Pitt the Younger), became Prime Minister in 1783. Pitt was a bright young man from the very beginning – he was called the 'Boy Patriot'. He entered Parliament as a member for the family pocket borough. At the time he was also a Cornet of Horse, a junior officer in the army. When Pitt made a brilliant speech supporting the Prince of Wales against his father, King George II, Walpole said, *'We must muzzle this terrible Cornet of Horse,'* and promptly had Pitt dismissed from the army. The muzzling didn't work. Pitt was taken up as a martyr by the army and if anything his political career was advanced.

He soon rose to be a dominating figure in Parliament. Like Walpole, Pitt was brought in to sort out a crisis. By now Britain was back at war with her old enemies the French. They were fighting over America and India, which both countries were trying to grab for themselves. Britain wasn't doing at all well, and Pitt was a leading critic of the weak and indecisive Government. He knew what should be done about it too. *'I can save this country, and no-one else can.'*

Taking him at his word, the Whig Duke of Devonshire persuaded the king to make the young Tory fire-eater Secretary of State.

VICTORIOUS PITT

Pitt was as good as his word. Unlike Walpole, who avoided aggro

THE IMPORTANCE OF TRADE IS SHOWN IN THE LORD CHANCELLOR'S SEAT
IN THE HOUSE OF LORDS - THE WOOLSACK - STUFFED WITH WOOL FROM
ALL OVER THE EMPIRE

abroad, Pitt was an imperialist and an expansionist. *When Trade is at stake you must defend it or perish.*

Pitt's policies met with almost immediate success. The brilliant young Robert Clive saw off the French at the Battle of Plassey, making the British top nation in India.

In America another of Pitt's bright young men, Major-General James Wolfe, defeated the French at the Heights of Abraham, capturing Quebec, and dying heroically in the battle.

In Europe Pitt did a deal with the warlike Prussian ruler, Frederick the Great. The Prussians would fight the French on the Continent, while the Brits took care of them at sea and abroad. In 1759 Pitt's troops defeated the French at the Battle of Minden, while the Navy won a victory at sea in the same year. Applauded by the people, and by the bankers and businessmen as well, Pitt was riding high. But there was trouble ahead. The royalty factor wasn't finished in British politics after all. A new king was about to make a comeback . . .

GEORGE TURNS BACK THE CLOCK

When George II died at the age of 76 he was succeeded not by his son Frederick, who had died ten years earlier, but by his grandson, who became King George III.

The new king was still young, only 22, tall and handsome, with an eye for the ladies. Born and raised in England, he was the first British king for ages without a thick German accent. He took an interest in agriculture, and was known to his affectionate subjects as Farmer George. King George III also had strong ideas on the position of the monarchy. In his eyes, previous monarchs, like Queen Anne and Georges I and II, had given up too much of the royal power too soon.

To be fair, George III didn't want to rule as a despot – but he was determined to make the monarchy a real power in politics once again. He dismissed Pitt and appointed a series of puppet Prime Ministers. Largely ignoring both Whigs and Tories, he created his own King's Party, which dominated Parliament. All in all, the new system didn't work out too well.

George III signed a treaty to end the war with France, throwing away many of Britain's gains in the process. There was a storm of protest. Pitt, worn out and ill, returned to Parliament to make a long speech condemning the treaty. *'We have given France the means of recovering her prodigious losses and becoming once more formidable to us at sea.'* Pitt had an unlikely ally. The treaty was also attacked by a radical journalist and politician called John Wilkes.

WILKES AND LIBERTY

Wilkes was an extraordinary figure, very much a symbol of the new age. He exemplified the growing power of Parliament and of the press. A journalist as well as an MP, Wilkes attacked the government and the too-powerful crown in his newspaper 'The New Briton'. Eventually he went too far, criticising the king in personal terms, and was thrown into jail. (Makes you wonder what they'd have done to some of today's tabloid editors.) Claiming immunity as an MP, Wilkes was soon released – and immediately demanded compensation. He got it too.

A lively and often scandalous figure, Wilkes was a member of the infamous 'Hell-Fire Club', whose aristocratic members were reputed to hold satanic orgies in the caves below Medmenham Abbey. Eventually he was thrown out of the Commons over a duel and went off to the Continent. Rumours of various amorous adventures came back to Britain. Then Wilkes himself returned, and actually had the cheek to get himself elected to Parliament again. The king was furious, and Wilkes was again expelled. He promptly got himself re-elected, only to be expelled once more. His supporters rioted with cries of *Wilkes and Liberty!* Wilkes was re-elected yet again. This time the Government disqualified him, insisting his opponent had won. Wilkes protested against the decision, the appeal was successful, and he was allowed to take his seat. A lively and troublesome MP for many years, he eventually turned respectable and ended up as Lord Mayor of London.

More of a Parliamentary gadfly than a major politician, Wilkes became a symbol for all those who opposed autocratic government. Raffish and disreputable, he wasn't the representative his fellow MPs might have chosen – but he was still an elected MP. As Pitt pointed out, if the Establishment was allowed to crush Wilkes, every other MP's liberty was at risk.

THE AMERICAN MUDDLE

Meanwhile, trouble was brewing in the American colonies. Britain wanted to tax the colonies to help pay for their defence. The Americans objected, setting up a cry of *'No taxation without representation!'*

At first the still-loyal colonists simply wanted a fairer deal, but George III's government handled them so badly that they were soon driven into outright rebellion, making their famous Declaration of Independence in 1776. The Government tried to crush the rebels – and made a mess of that as well. There followed a long and thoroughly mis-managed war, with several missed opportunities for a settlement, or even for victory. Britain's enemies rushed to join in on the American side. Soon Britain was fighting not only America, but France and the Netherlands too. The situation was hopeless.

In 1782 George Washington forced British troops to surrender at Yorktown. In 1783 the British signed a treaty at Versailles, recognising America's independence.

GEORGE PAYS THE PRICE

Back home people were shocked and horrified by Britain's defeat. What's more, everyone knew who to blame – George III and his new-fangled, or rather old-fangled, King's Party. The House of Commons, determined to regain control, passed an indignant resolution that *'The influence of the Crown has increased, is increasing, and ought to diminish.'*

The king was well aware of the national feeling, and actually considered abdication. Like France, the country seemed on the brink of revolution. The situation was saved by a general election, and a determined return to the two-party system.

YOUNG MR PITT

Once more a political saviour turned up, in the youthful form of Pitt the Younger. Son of the now ennobled Pitt the Elder, young Mr Pitt was something of a child prodigy. He went to Cambridge at 14, was an MP by the time he was 20, and Prime Minister at the age of 24.

A brilliant politician, he was cold and stiff in manner, with few social graces. *'Smiles are not natural to him,'* said a fellow MP. Pitt's most pressing worries as Prime Minister were mainly financial. The country was broke (nothing changes, does it?), bankrupted by the expense of the American war. Pitt was forced to raise taxes. He even put a tax on houses with more than seven windows. (Some people just bricked the extra windows up.) Pitt encouraged trade as well, and even signed a commercial treaty with Britain's old enemy France.

TO AVOID PAYING THE NEW WINDOW TAX, MANY PEOPLE HAD THEIR
WINDOWS BRICKED IN

AND THIS I TAKE IT
IS THE GREEN HOUSE

COMES THE REVOLUTION

In 1789, France erupted in revolution.

To begin with at least, the French Revolution had lots of support amongst progressively-minded British intellectuals. It was seen, rightly enough, as the overthrow of an unjust and tyrannical system. Poets and the more radical politicians went overboard for the new revolutionary ideals of *'Liberty, Equality, Fraternity!' 'Bliss it was that dawn to be alive,'* rhapsodised the young Wordsworth. *'And to be young was very heaven.'* Charles James Fox, leader of the Whig opposition, declared it to be *'the greatest event that had happened in the world'*.

But as the French Revolution got under way, the British started to have second thoughts. It was bad enough when the revolutionaries started cutting off the heads of the nobility. When the French executed their king the British were shocked and outraged – even though they'd done exactly the same thing a hundred years earlier.

FEARS RAN HIGH THAT THE FRENCH REVOLUTION WOULD FIND ITS WAY TO BRITAIN

The British Parliament still consisted largely of the aristocracy, their relations and their followers. Worried in case the fashion for head-lopping spread across the Channel, Parliament passed a number of repressive measures, banning seditious writings and meetings. Pro-revolutionary societies were suppressed, and the newly-emerging Trade Unions were banned. Even meeting to talk about your wages became illegal.

THE PEASANTS ARE REVOLTING!

France's continental neighbours, equally horrified, sent in troops to put a stop to all this nonsense. Not only did the republicans refuse to be put down, but their ragged revolutionary armies actually started conquering their attackers. Soon France had occupied Belgium, and was threatening most of Europe.

In 1793 Britain declared war on France. The two countries were to be at war, on and off, for the next 20-odd years. (The war ground to a halt in 1801, when it was ended, temporarily, by the Peace of Amiens – but both sides knew it was really only half-time.)

UP THE IRISH!

In the same year Pitt, who had proved to be a highly efficient war-time Prime Minister, resigned over Ireland, a country causing almost as much trouble as France.

The unlucky Irish had been struggling unsuccessfully for their freedom for hundreds of years. In an attempt to break the cycle of rebellions followed by reprisals, Pitt decided that Ireland should become officially part of Britain. Dublin's Parliament merged with that of Westminster and the so-called United Kingdom was born.

In 1801 an Act of Union was passed. In future the Irish were to return members to the British Parliament. But although Irish

Catholics, unlike British ones, were now allowed to vote, they were still forbidden to sit in Parliament. Since the majority of the Irish were Catholic, this was greatly resented. Those who had been active in the Dublin Parliament were now excluded from the British one.

Recognising the injustice, Pitt attempted to introduce a measure giving Catholics the right to sit in Parliament. It was blocked by George III, who felt this would mean breaking the royal promise, given at his Coronation, to protect the Protestant religion.

Worn out by attempting to deal with the war, the king and the Irish all together, Pitt resigned.

PEACE AND WAR

Since Britain was now at peace, the new Prime Minister, Henry Addison, started disarming, and British tourists flocked over to France.

A year later the war was on again and Napoleon was building a fleet of invasion barges at Boulogne. Addison just couldn't cope, and the nation demanded Pitt, who returned as Prime Minister in 1804. After two more years of desperate struggle against a seemingly invincible Napoleon, Pitt died in 1806, worn out by ill health and over-work. Not long before his death, he attended the Lord Mayor's dinner, where he was hailed as the Saviour of Europe. Modestly Pitt replied, *'England has saved herself by her exertions and the rest of Europe will be saved by her example.'*

NAPOLEON'S WATERLOO

The war dragged on for nine more weary years. Gradually the tide turned. In 1815 the Duke of Wellington, leading the armies of

Britain and her allies, finally defeated Napoleon at the Battle of Waterloo in 1815. A new age was about to begin.

REACTION AND REFORM

After the victory at Waterloo, Britain became the leading power in Europe. With her growing Empire, she was soon to dominate the world. Back home however, there were problems, not solved by the war but simply postponed, which just had to be faced.

With the Industrial Revolution came the emergence of a powerful new middle class. The lives of the poor were affected too. People were moving from country villages to big towns. Factory workers' living conditions, both at work and at home, were often shockingly bad.

Britain had been at war, on and off, for 22 years. As always in war-time, authoritarian attitudes had hardened. Reformers had been treated like revolutionaries, and any opposition to the Government was seen as treason. Once the war was over, the reform movement started to get going again. A major issue was the widespread demand for the reform of Parliament.

RIOTS AND RUMPUSES

A radical journalist called William Cobbett began holding mass meetings. There were all kinds of riots and demonstrations. In the industrial north the Luddites, militant men put out of work by new machinery, started smashing up factories. Near London a huge crowd assembled in Spa Fields and had to be dispersed by police. Unemployed workers from Manchester, called the Blanketeers, led a march on London.

THE LUDDITE RIOTS WERE A PREDICTABLE RESPONSE TO THE INDUSTRIAL REVOLUTION

PETERLOO

In 1819 a large crowd gathered in St Peters Fields outside Manchester to hear a speech by a radical MP called Henry Hunt. Known because of his eloquence as 'Orator Hunt' he was a keen advocate of Parliamentary reform.

So large and rowdy was the crowd that local magistrates panicked and ordered Henry Hunt to be arrested. They called out the troops and the cavalry charged the crowd. Eleven of the demonstrators were killed, many more were hurt. The incident became known as the Peterloo Massacre, in a mocking reference to the recent battle of Waterloo.

Next year, to make matters even worse, a group of radical extremists plotted another massacre in revenge. Called the Cato

Street Conspiracy, it was a plan to assassinate all the members of the Cabinet and seize power. Before anything actually happened the plot was discovered, the conspirators were caught and the four ringleaders executed.

Thoroughly alarmed, the Government passed the Six Acts, which included measures limiting the freedom of the Press, curtailing the right to hold public meetings, and giving the magistrates extra powers.

TIME FOR CHANGE

Despite all this repression, pressure for change was growing. Younger, more liberal politicians began appearing in Parliament. One of them was Sir Robert Peel. He was a member of the newly-powerful middle class, the son of a wealthy cotton manufacturer. In his time as Home Secretary, Peel reformed the law, abolishing the death penalty for over 100 offences. He set up

PEEL ABOLISHED THE DEATH PENALTY FOR MORE THAN A
HUNDRED OFFENCES

"IT'S HARD, ISN'T IT, COPING WITH
THESE FEELINGS OF REJECTION"

Britain's first proper police force. The new police were nicknamed 'Bobbies', or 'Peelers', after their creator, names which survive to the present day.

ENTER THE DUKE

The political parties were still in a pretty fluid state with lots of chopping and changing and ever-shifting alliances. In 1827 there were four Prime Ministers in one year. The fourth was the Duke of Wellington, a much revered military hero, and, as you might expect, a firmly reactionary old Tory. Peel found himself the only liberal politician left in the Cabinet.

CATHOLIC EMANCIPATION

Nevertheless, the reformers were starting to make some progress, particularly in the area of Catholic emancipation – the freeing of Catholics from the many restrictions imposed on them by the Protestant state. Left over from the historical struggles between the two religions, these restrictions meant Catholics were forbidden to attend university, to vote in elections, to become MPs, or to hold public office.

This led to an absurd situation in Ireland, whose Parliament had been merged with Britain's in 1801. In 1827, Daniel O'Connell, a popular Irish politician, was elected to Parliament – but couldn't take his seat since he was a Catholic. The Irish were naturally furious and the situation in Ireland, never very peaceful at the best of times, started to look very ugly.

The Duke of Wellington was too good a soldier not to know when to retreat. He joined with Peel in backing an Emancipation Bill. There was tremendous opposition from the Protestant British, still suspicious of any increase in Catholic power, and the king, now

31

George IV, even threatened to abdicate. But Wellington forced the bill through, and in 1829 it became law. As a result, 60 Irish MPs entered Parliament, livening up the old place no end.

FORCING THE CATHOLIC EMANCIPATION BILL THROUGH GAVE
WELLINGTON THE GREATEST DIFFICULTY

COMPARED TO THIS,
WATERLOO WAS
A SNIP!

ELECTORAL REFORM

By now Parliamentary reform was well overdue. Although Parliament resembled the institution we know today, in many ways it was very different. Britain had about 10 million inhabitants, and only half a million of them met the property-owning qualifications which gave them the right to vote. Parliament itself was still effectively run by the powerful noblemen in the House of Lords.

Wellington's lapse into liberalism lost him the confidence of his party and he was forced out of office. The new king, William IV, asked the Whig politician Earl Grey (the one they named the tea after) to take office. The Earl wasn't too keen. He reckoned Britain was ripe for revolution. At last he agreed – but only if the king promised to back a Reform Bill.

THE KING COMES UP TRUMPS

The king agreed and the bill went forward – but not very far. The Tory opposition fought it like mad, and the House of Lords blocked it completely. Earl Grey asked the king to create enough new peers to get the Bill passed. Going back on his promise, the king refused; Grey demanded an election. The king's advisors said it was too short notice. Ignoring them the king marched into Parliament – in such a hurry that his crown was on crooked – and read out the speech dissolving Parliament.

The new election gave the reforming Whigs an even bigger majority – but the House of Lords remained as obstinate as ever. The Lords blocked the bill yet again – and rioting broke out all over the country. For once revolution really did seem close. Finally keeping his promise, the king threatened to create 50 new peers, enough to swamp the Lords with supporters of reform. The Lords backed down. In July 1832 the first Reform Bill was passed.

RESULTS OF REFORM

Today you might well wonder what all the fuss was about. The Bill abolished some of the tinier constituencies and created new ones to cover under-represented areas. It increased the franchise, the right to vote, to '£10 freeholders' – the owners of land or property worth £10 per annum; big money in those days.

Both Whigs and Tories still only represented people with money and land – neither side was in favour of anything so extreme as giving the ordinary man a vote – and as for women . . . Neverther-less, the Reform Bill had huge symbolic importance. By responding, even in a limited way, to public pressure, the king, Parliament and the Lords had given the reformers enough hope to prevent a violent revolution. The pot was still bubbling away – but at least the Government had stopped trying to sit on the lid. (They'd seen what that led to in France.)

The new Parliament began a series of much-needed reforms. Slavery was finally abolished in British colonies, not before time. A number of Factory Acts were passed. Children weren't allowed to

work in factories until they were at least nine years old, and even then they weren't allowed to work more than nine hours a day. These and other liberal regulations annoyed the newly-rich manufacturing magnates no end. How could they be expected to make a decent profit if they weren't allowed to grind the faces of the poor?

It's an attitude that hasn't entirely disappeared . . .

PARLIAMENT'S NEW HOME

IN 1834 THE OLD PALACE BURNED DOWN

TOO MUCH HOT AIR

In 1834 Parliament lost its old home. Much of the Palace of Westminster was destroyed in a fire. The present Houses of Parliament, designed by Sir Thomas Barry, were built over the next 30 years.

THE NEW PARLIAMENT BUILDING TOOK 30 YEARS TO COMPLETE

THE DICKENS OF AN ELECTION

In his youth, the novelist Charles Dickens served his time as a Parliamentary reporter.

For long hours he crouched in the Press Gallery, taking down endless long-winded speeches in shorthand. At election time he was whirled round the country by stage coach, dashing off his account of the campaign in some lonely hotel room while the courier waited to gallop back to London with his copy. It has to be said that this experience gave Dickens a life-long scorn for politicians and all their works.

In 'Pickwick Papers', his first, best-selling novel, Dickens gives a hilarious account of an election of the time. Mr Pickwick and his friends go down to the little town of Eatanswill to witness the contest between the Honourable Samuel Slumkey, the Blue candidate, and Horatio Fizkin for the Buff party. (Presumably Blues and Buffs stand for Tories and Whigs, though Dickens doesn't bother to specify. To him one lot of politicians was very much like another.)

As soon as they arrive they are surrounded by a rowdy mob screaming *'Slumkey forever! No Fizkin!'*

Mr Pickwick joins in the shouting, telling his friends, *'It's always best on these occasions to do what the mob do.'* *'Suppose there are two mobs?'* asks someone nervously. *'Shout with the largest,'* replies Mr Pickwick.

They meet Mr Perker, election agent for the Blues, who gives them a lesson in practical politics. *'We have opened all the public houses in the place and left our adversary nothing but the beer shops,'* he tells them proudly. *'Masterly stroke of policy that.'*

However, despite this brilliant coup, the result of the election is still in the balance. *'Fizkin's people have got three and thirty voters in the lock-up coach house at the White Heart. They keep 'em locked up there till they want 'em . . . to prevent our getting at them; and even if we could it would be no use for they keep them very drunk on purpose. Smart fellow,*

Fizkin's agent – very smart fellow indeed.'

But Mr Perker isn't beaten. He has presented the ladies of the town with green parasols. Women don't have the vote of course, but the little present has *'secured all their husbands and half their brothers'*.

Meanwhile Sam Weller, Mr Pickwick's servant, is helping to sober up voters who've been celebrating too enthusiastically. *'We dragged 'em out one by one this morning and put 'em under the pump . . . shilling a head the Committee paid for that.'* Last year, Sam tells the shocked Mr Pickwick, the opposition party bribed a barmaid to *'hocus'* the brandy and water of some loyal voters by drugging it with laudanum.

'Blessed if she didn't send 'em to sleep till twelve hours arter the election was over. They took one man up to the booth fast asleep by way of experiment, but it was no go – they wouldn't poll him; so they brought him back and put him to bed again.' (In 1837, true incorruptible parliamentary democracy was still quite a way away.)

Later Mr Pickwick and his friends are in the crowd as the candidate, the Honourable Samuel Slumkey, comes out to greet the waiting crowd.

'Suddenly the crowd set up a great cheering.

"He has come out," said little Mr Perker.

Another cheer, much louder.

"He has shaken hands with the men," cried the little agent.

Another cheer, far more vehement.

"He has patted the babies on the head," said Mr Perker, trembling with anxiety.

A roar of applause rent the air.

"He has kissed one of 'em!" exclaimed the delighted little man.

A second roar.

"He has kissed another," gasped the excited manager.

A third roar.

"He's kissing 'em all!" screamed the enthusiastic little gentleman. And hailed by the deafening shouts of the multitude, the procession moved on.'

In politics, some things at least never change. Pickwick Papers was published in book form in 1837 – the year that Queen Victoria came to the throne . . .

VICTORIAN TIMES

ENGLAND'S NEW QUEEN

William IV had no direct male heir. When he died in 1837 the throne passed to his 18-year-old niece Victoria. (Her father, the Duke of Kent, had died when she was a baby.) The Victorian age had begun. Britain was rich and powerful, new industries flourished, and the British Empire was spreading all over the world.

Victoria was to reign for the next 64 years, right up to the beginning of the twentieth century. She came to the throne as a young girl of 18, after a sheltered and secluded life. Her mother had kept her away from Court, saying, probably quite rightly, that it was a den of iniquity, and had even insisted on sleeping in the young princess's room.

But young Victoria had a strong will and a decided personality of her own. On her very first day as queen she excluded her mother from her first Council meeting – and that night she had mum's bed moved out.

From a shy young queen, Victoria developed into a much-loved monarch, ending up, after her incredibly long reign, as a formidable old lady, Rudyard Kipling's 'Widow of Windsor'. Respectability was the keynote of Victoria's reign. Earlier monarchs had sometimes been a pretty raffish lot, tyrannical, drunken, lecherous, sometimes downright loony, but there was none of that nonsense about Victoria.

Soon after her coronation she married her cousin Albert of Saxe-Coburg-Gotha, a serious-minded German prince. (Albert is credited with introducing the Christmas tree custom to Britain.) As well as a queen, Victoria was a devoted wife and mother and the royal couple had nine children, four boys and five girls. The monarchy came to symbolise the importance of a stable and respectable family life. (Some of our present lot must be throwbacks to the bad old days . . .)

POLITICS AND THE QUEEN

Queen Victoria could be called our first really modern monarch. Although she had strong opinions, and often gave her ministers a hard time, she eventually accepted the principle that her role was to give advice not orders. Though that's not how she started out . . .

Victoria was greatly influenced by the fatherly Lord Melbourne, the Whig Prime Minister in the early years of her reign. When Melbourne was defeated in 1839, Sir Robert Peel tried to put together a Tory government. He got off to a bad start by ordering Victoria to get rid of her Ladies of the Bedchamber, a group of aristocratic ladies who traditionally attended the queen. This particular lot were all Whigs, and he feared their influence on the young queen.

Strong-minded from the start, Victoria refused. She didn't want to part with her ladies – and she didn't want to lose Melbourne either. She persuaded him to stay on as Prime Minister, and he survived for two more years. But when the election of 1841 gave the Tories a clear majority, Peel said that the queen *must* choose a Prime Minister who commanded a majority in the Commons.

Queen Victoria gave way and Lord Melbourne had to step down. It was an important constitutional victory, and a further step towards the Parliament we know today.

MELBOURNE, VICTORIA'S FAVOURITE PM, DID NOT COMMAND A MAJORITY IN THE HOUSE

PEEL AND THE CHARTISTS

In his second Ministry – he'd been Prime Minister, very briefly, in 1834 – Peel had to face the problem of the Chartists, an early working class movement that had grown up out of hard times. They complained that they were bowed down under taxes and that workmen were starving. *'Capital brings no reward, the workhouse is full and the factory deserted.'* (Sounds all too familiar, doesn't it?)

The Chartists had over 100 branches and their meetings drew huge crowds. They took their name from their demand for a 'People's Charter'. (Must be where John Major got the idea.) They demanded votes for everyone (well, men anyway), a secret ballot, equal-sized electoral districts, wages for MPs, the abolition of the property qualifications for MPs and voters, and general elections every year.

Today all these rights, except for the last one, are taken for granted. At the time they were seen as madly revolutionary ideas.

RAIN STOPS PLAY

The Chartists presented giant petitions to Parliament, all of which were turned down. Most Chartists were moderates who wanted to work through Parliament. When all their attempts failed, certain extremists began talking about *'wading to freedom through rivers of blood'*.

There were a number of Chartist-inspired riots, and in 1848, with revolutions going on all over the Continent, the Chartists planned to march on Parliament with a monster petition bearing two million signatures. Britain was saved from revolution by the weather. On the appointed day it was pouring with rain. The march fizzled out and the petition was peacefully delivered by cab . . .

IN THE END, THE CHARTIST REVOLUTION FIZZLED OUT, AND THE PETITION WAS DELIVERED BY CAB

REFORM AT LAST

Although the Chartists didn't get far with their petitions, Peel's government did put through a number of important reforms. These included the Mines Act, another Factory Act, and the first Public Health Act. Most important of all, in 1846 Peel reformed the Corn Laws, which had penalised the poor by keeping the price of wheat, and therefore bread, artificially high.

LIBS V TORIES

Around this time the always-cloudy party divisions get even more confused. Peel's repeal of the Corn Laws had split the Tory party into 'Peelites', Peel's loyal supporters, and Protectionists, led by the up-and-coming Disraeli. Eventually the parties sorted themselves out into two groups.

Disraeli's lot eventually became known as Conservatives, the old hard-line Tories under a new and more respectable-sounding name. On the other side was a mixture of Peelites and Whigs, including reform-minded radical MPs, lumped together under the name of Liberals.

BOLD BAD PAM

One of the most colourful political figures of this rather mixed-up period was Viscount Palmerston, known to his many admirers and enemies as 'Pam'.

Foreign Secretary 1830–1841 and 1846–1851, and Prime Minister 1855–1865, Palmerston was a sort of hangover from the more dashing days of the eighteenth century. Although a Liberal, Pam believed in an aggressive foreign policy, vigorously defending British interests all over the world. Any hint of trouble from stroppy foreigners and Pam would bellow, '*Send a gunboat!*' If the crafty foreigners were unsporting enough to be land-locked, he would send a military expeditionary force instead.

CHARGE!

All this red-blooded John Bull patriotism went down a bomb with the Great British Public. They were particularly pleased with Pam's successful leadership in the Crimean war. This was a confused conflict between Britain, allied this time with her old enemy France, and the Russians, who were starting to challenge Britain's power.

PALMERSTON'S ENTHUSIASM FOR WAR LED US INTO THE DISASTROUS CRIMEA CAMPAIGN

Until Pam took over as PM, things hadn't been going too well.

This was the war that produced that legendary heroic cock-up known as the Charge of the Light Brigade, a brave but suicidal dash by a troop of British cavalry – straight at the Russian guns.

PASSIONATE PAM

But if the flamboyant Pam was popular with the public, he didn't go down at all well with Queen Victoria. She disapproved of his aggressive foreign policy, and even more of his fondness for wine, women and song.

What really put the lid on it was his alleged attack on one of her ladies-in-waiting, carried out, shock, horror, in the royal residence of Windsor Castle itself. Pam's version of events was that one of the ladies-in-waiting was eagerly awaiting his late-night visit. Slightly fuddled by the after-dinner port, he'd found himself in the wrong bedroom. Could have happened to anybody – but as far as Victoria was concerned it was attempted rape.

Prince Albert didn't believe Palmerston's story either. According to him, Palmerston *would have consummated his fiendish scheme by violence, had not the miraculous efforts of his victim and such assistance attracted by her screams saved her . . .'* Luckily for Palmerston, the all-powerful Lord Melbourne was his brother-in-law. To prevent a family scandal Melbourne hushed everything up, but Queen Victoria never forgot . . .

Pam was still making passes at the ladies well into his eighties. His other appetites were pretty powerful as well. At a Parliamentary dinner the amazed Speaker of the House watched Pam tuck into turtle soup, cod with oyster sauce, pâté, two entrees, roast mutton, ham and pheasant . . .

Today's tabloids would have really loved Pam.

DISRAELI v GLADSTONE

After Palmerston died in 1865, politics became a struggle between two of the most famous names in parliamentary history, the Conservative leader Disraeli, and the Liberal leader, Gladstone. They dominated politics for the rest of the century, and for most of the time they took it in turns to be Prime Minister. It would be hard to imagine a more completely contrasting pair of politicians.

DEBONAIR DIZZY

Benjamin Disraeli must be one of the most unlikely Prime Ministers in British politics. In a class-prejudiced age, when your average MP, let alone your average PM, was probably some kind of aristocrat, Disraeli was a complete outsider. The son of a Spanish Jew, he was baptised a Christian when still a boy. Disraeli was handsome, charming, witty, and something of a dandy. He was intelligent and artistic as well, and the author of such successful novels as 'Vivian Grey', 'Sybil' and 'Coningsby'. (*When I want to read a good novel, I write one!*' said Dizzy.) How Disraeli ever rose to the leadership of the Conservative party with all these handicaps is something of a mystery. (Even today, one of the most damaging things one Tory can say about another is to accuse him of being 'too clever by half'.) Even Disraeli was rather surprised by his own success. When he first became PM he remarked, *'I have climbed to the top of the greasy pole.'*

DIZZY AND VICTORIA

Disraeli had one big advantage over his Liberal rival. The monarch, although less powerful, was still tremendously influential – and Queen Victoria thought Disraeli was simply wonderful. Disraeli had an infallible method of dealing with the queen. *'Everyone likes flattery, and when you come to royalty you should lay it on with a trowel.'*

After the death of her beloved husband Prince Albert in 1861, Victoria had gone into deep mourning and semi-retirement. The Great British Public, fed up with having a queen who was never seen, was beginning to wonder if the monarchy was worth keeping. (The very opposite of today, when we seem to see far too much of some of our royals . . .)

Disraeli coaxed the queen into resuming her public engagements, and she soon became a much-loved monarch once more. She was particularly pleased when Disraeli arranged for her to be created Empress of India in 1876. Feeling, no doubt, that one good title deserved another, she created him Earl of Beaconsfield.

GRIM GLADSTONE

William Ewart Gladstone the Liberal leader was a very different type, as solid and serious as his name. Deeply religious, he tended to think that his plans and God's will were pretty much the same thing.

Victoria couldn't stand him. *'He speaks to me,'* she once said, *'as if I was a public meeting.'*

GLADSTONE AND QUEEN VICTORIA

"YES, MA'AM, I'D LOVE
ANOTHER CUP!"

Late for a royal rendezvous, Gladstone made things worse by trying to pass it off with a snappy joke. He had three hands, he said, *'a left hand, a right hand, and a little behind-hand'*. Queen Victoria's reply has passed into the language. *'We are not amused,'* she said.

She would have been even less amused had she known about Gladstone's habit of roaming the streets late at night having long conversations with ladies of the town. He said he was only wrestling with their souls, trying to convert them to the path of virtue. Knowing Gladstone that's probably exactly what he was doing. But it's a story those still-uninvented tabloids would have revelled in . . .

REFORM ROLLS ON

Disraeli and Gladstone frequently clashed in Parliament, and here too Disraeli had the advantage. Cool and detached by nature, he was often able to run rings round the more emotional Gladstone. As Lord Stanley put it, *'Gladstone's temper is visible and audible whenever he rises to speak . . . the mixture of anger and contempt in his voice is almost painful to witness. With all his splendid talent and his great position, few men suffer more from the constitutional infirmity of an irritable nature. Disraeli is quite aware of the advantage he possesses in his natural calmness . . .'*

Despite the contrast of their personalities, their policies weren't wildly different. Both carried on the prevailing trend towards reform.

Gladstone's government brought in reforms in education and the civil service.

Disraeli's administration passed Acts to improve public health, factory conditions and the safety of shipping, and granted legal recognition to trade unions, a measure which was to have great effect in the future. It also passed one of the first truly Green measures, a law prohibiting the dumping of industrial waste in rivers. There may have been a bit of enlightened self-interest here.

The new Houses of Parliament overlooked the river – and in those days, the Thames ponged so much in hot summers that it was known as The Great Stink . . .

HER MAJESTY'S LOYAL OPPOSITION

"WE ON THIS SIDE OF THE HOUSE
SEE NO EVIDENCE OF POLLUTION
IN THE THAMES WHATSOEVER"

VOTERS GALORE

Perhaps the most important reforms were those concerning Parliament itself.

In 1867 the Conservatives passed the second Reform Act. The

number of those entitled to vote rose from 1.36 million to 2.46 million, almost double.

In 1872 the secret ballot, one of the old Chartist demands, finally became law.

THE IMPORTANCE OF SECRET BALLOTS

Keeping up the good work, the Liberals passed a third Reform Act in 1884, extending the franchise to all householders and so increasing the number of voters to 5.7 million. By now four out of five adult males had the vote. (An even more revolutionary idea, votes for women, was being urged by such early 'suffragists', as Millicent Fawcett.)

As the electorate expanded, both parties had to think more about representing the people of Britain, rather than a particular group of the rich and powerful.

UP THE IRISH! (AGAIN)

One of the biggest problems for the politicians of Britain was the politics of Ireland. Continually mishandled by its British rulers, Ireland became a problem that just wouldn't go away. (It still hasn't.) Although there might be peace for a time, 'the Troubles' always flared up again.

DIZZY'S DUEL

Disraeli got involved in Irish affairs even before he was an MP. Standing as parliamentary candidate for Taunton in 1835 he was alleged to have described the Irish MP Daniel O'Connell as *'an incendiary and a traitor'*.

O'Connell retaliated by making a speech in Dublin in which he called Disraeli *'a liar both in action and words'* and suggested that he was probably a direct descendant of *'the impenitent thief on the cross'* – a reference to Disraeli's Jewish ancestry.

This was fighting talk – but Daniel O'Connell had once killed a man in a duel, and had sworn never to fight another. On a previous occasion Daniel's son Morgan had fought a duel on his father's behalf. So the fiery young Disraeli challenged Morgan to a duel. Morgan, however, had no intention of fighting everyone his father annoyed, and declined the invitation. Disraeli wrote a rude letter to Daniel, calling him *'a Yahoo'* and an even ruder one to Morgan challenging him, or any of his relatives, to take up the quarrel if they dared. A few mornings later, as Disraeli wrote in a letter to his sister, *'I was lying in bed, thankful that I had kicked all the O'Connells, when the police officer of Marylebone rushed into my chamber and took me into custody.'* One of O'Connell's friends had sworn a complaint, and Disraeli was bound over to keep the peace *'in £500 sureties'*.

Disraeli, who loved publicity, was quite happy with this result.

'Row with the O'Connells,' he wrote in his diary, *'in which I greatly distinguish myself.'*

GLADSTONE FIGHTS FOR PEACE

When Gladstone became PM in 1868 he was determined to pacify Ireland. His government passed the Irish Church Act, which meant that the Catholic Irish no longer had to pay for a Protestant church they didn't want. The Irish Land Act of 1870 was intended to protect tenants against oppressive landlords and excessive rents. But the Act failed to define 'excessive' properly, and it just didn't work.

The disappointed Irish got stroppy again, violence broke out and in 1871 Gladstone had to pass a Coercion Act, giving the police more powers and sending more troops. (It's something of a tribute to the fighting qualities of the Irish that more British troops were needed to hold down Ireland than the whole of India!) Ireland remained a perpetual problem. There were six different governments between 1880 and 1895, and four of them fell because of Ireland.

A lot of the confusion was caused by the 80 Irish MPs in the British Parliament. Determined to achieve Home Rule they voted with whichever party they thought would help them most, causing quite a bit of chaos and splitting the Liberal Party into Liberals (who were pro Home Rule) and Liberal Unionists (who were against it).

Finally the Irish question brought down the great Gladstone himself. Over the years Gladstone had had so much trouble with the Irish that he was determined to get rid of them. Home Rule, he decided, was the only answer. In 1893 he got a Home Rule Bill past the Commons, only to have it turned down by the Lords. In 1894 Gladstone resigned, and in 1895 an alliance of Conservatives and

Liberal Unionists took power. Gladstone's attempts to solve the Irish problem had failed.

HERE'S KEIR!

There was another political force on the parliamentary horizon, small as yet but immensely important for the future. The workers were beginning to get organised.

Ever since the 1850s 'New Model' Unions had been forming themselves mostly for skilled workers. At first they simply concentrated on improving their working conditions, but as time went on they realised that if they were really going to achieve anything, they needed to get working men represented in Parliament.

In 1868 the first meeting of the Trades Union Congress, a sort of union of unions, took place in Manchester. One of its resolutions was 'to take action in all parliamentary actions pertaining to the working class'.

The unions formed an alliance with the new Independent Labour Party, formed in 1889 by a fighting Scottish socialist called Keir Hardie.

Keir had been a coalminer from the age of ten, so he knew all about the problems of the workers. By the time he was 22 he got fired for being an agitator. He became a union organiser, and eventually secretary of the Scottish Miners Federation. A keen socialist, Keir came up with a revolutionary idea. It was no use the workers relying on well-meaning middle class Liberals to help them. They had to have a party of their own. So Keir founded one.

Three years later, Keir Hardie became the first Labour MP. He didn't sneak shyly into Parliament either – he wanted people to know that the first of the workers had arrived. So Keir Hardie turned up to take his seat at Westminster 'in a toil-stained working suit with a cloth cap on his head and accompanied by a noisy brass band!'

WAR WITH THE BOERS

Earlier struggles over America and India between the great powers had been followed by a similar 'Scramble for Africa'. In 1899 a nasty little colonial uprising called the Boer War broke out. The might of Britain was opposed by a little group of Afrikaaner guerillas (called Boers) – and the public was badly shaken when the rebels scored three quick victories on the trot. Britain won in the end (of course) but only after a long and costly campaign.

The Boers fought a sort of hit-and-run war in small swift-moving groups called commandos, and the British Army couldn't cope with opponents who refused to stay still.

Eventually the rebellious Boers, and their wives and families, were rounded up into places called 'concentration camps', where they were kept under harsh conditions behind barbed wire. Unlike Hitler's horrible establishments in World War Two these camps weren't designed to kill – but all the same by the end of the war 20,000 Boers had died in them from disease brought on by overcrowding and poor nourishment.

Opinion at home was outraged. In Parliament the Liberal leader Sir Henry Campbell-Bannerman said the war was being fought by *methods of barbarism*. Eventually Britain had to fork out three million pounds to rebuild the Boer farms that her own troops had destroyed.

PARTY TIME

Politically things were pretty confused. Liberals and Conservatives still formed the two main parties. But there were also shifting alliances between splinter groups calling themselves Whigs, Tories, Liberal Unionists, Liberal Radicals, Tory Democrats, Unionists, Labour, Liberal Labour and Irish Nationalists – not forgetting Keir Hardie and his Independent Labour brass band!

FAREWELL VICTORIA

In 1897 nationwide rejoicing celebrated Victoria's Diamond Jubilee – 60 years on the throne. Things were still looking good for Britain and the Empire, but change was on the way. In 1901 the old queen died, and the nation mourned. Britain, and its Parliament, prepared to face the challenges and problems of the twentieth century.

THE TWENTIETH CENTURY

EDWARD THE CARESSER

Queen Victoria was followed by her son Edward, who became King Edward VII. Poor old Teddy had spent so long waiting in the wings as a Prince of Wales (sound familiar?) that he took the throne as a rather portly 59-year-old gentleman, with a well-developed taste for champagne, gambling and the company of beautiful ladies.

ENTENTE TRES CORDIALE

An earlier, more piously-minded king had been known as Edward the Confessor. This one was affectionately nicknamed Edward the Caresser. Edward VII took little interest in politics, happy to play the role of constitutional monarch. He was a leading supporter of the new Entente Cordiale – an alliance with our old enemies, the French – and helped it along by frequent trips to Paris – strictly for diplomatic purposes of course . . .

NEW FACES

Politically things were changing fast. Most of the old Victorian heavyweights were gone by now, and new names were coming forward – names like Winston Churchill who became a Conservative MP in 1901, changed over to the Liberals in 1904, and then later rejoined the Conservatives. (Charged with treachery, Churchill said anyone could rat, but it took real talent to re-rat!)

Another up-and-coming talent was the fiery Welshman Lloyd George, a radical Liberal, who had been fiercely opposed to the Boer War.

FEARLESS ARTHUR

The Conservatives had been in power for the last seven years, and they held on to the reins in 1902, when A J Balfour became PM. Arthur Balfour was a cool, unflappable Scot, who'd made his name in the ever-stormy post of Irish Secretary. Once, during an especially heated debate, an angry Irish MP threatened to thump him, brandishing his fist under Balfour's nose. According to the young Winston Churchill who witnessed the scene, Balfour was quite fearless and *regarded the frantic figure with no more and no less than the interest of a biologist examining through a microscope the contortions of a rare and provoked insect*.

KILLING WITH KINDNESS

Balfour was against Irish Home Rule, planning, he said, to *'kill it with kindness'*. He was going to make the Irish so happy that they wouldn't want to separate from Britain. (Some hopes!) Balfour passed a reforming new Education Act, making the newly created County Councils responsible for education. (His other claim to fame is the Balfour Declaration of 1917, promising the Jewish people a homeland of their own in Palestine. Although the promise wasn't actually kept at the time, the declaration was one of the first steps towards the creation of the still-troubled state of Israel.)

A LIBERAL LANDSLIDE

The election of 1906 produced a Liberal landslide, and the Liberal leader Campbell-Bannerman became PM. (A big man in every sense of the word, 'C-B' as he was known, was a hearty eater, who weighed over 20 stone – as did his beloved wife Charlotte.)

The same election produced no less than 50 Labour MPs – Keir Hardie wasn't so lonely any more!

THE PEOPLE'S BUDGET

In 1908, Herbert Asquith, Campbell-Bannerman's Chancellor of the Exchequer, took over as Prime Minister, leading the Liberal Party in an important constitutional battle.

The Liberals had come to power keen on reform, but they were constantly blocked by the Lords – who were of course Conservatives to a man – or rather to a Lord. Every time the Liberals brought in some progressive legislation, the Lords sent it right back. A few minor reforms got through, like school meals in 1906. (That's a reform?) But many more were thrown out. Things came

LLOYD GEORGE - THE WELSH WIZARD

to a crunch in 1909 when Lloyd George, by now Chancellor of the Exchequer, brought in what he called his 'People's Budget'. This proposed a swingeing tax on the very rich to produce money not only for more reforms but for battleships as well. The British were getting nervous about the way the Germans were building up their navy.

LLOYD GEORGE IN TROUBLE

This was a particularly tricky time for Lloyd George. Like many another married politician, he was known to stray from time to time. (It's the stress, you know.) Just as he was preparing one of the most controversial budgets in history, he was accused by the 'People' newspaper of being involved in an affair with a married woman – a far bigger scandal then than it is today. Lloyd George knew that if he didn't deny the story and sue the newspaper as well his career would be ruined. The trouble was, the story in the 'People' was perfectly true. A born politician, Lloyd George didn't hesitate for a moment. He went into the witness box and lied under oath. Not only that, he persuaded his wife, who knew all about the affair, to give him public support. *'One day I shall be Prime Minister,'* he told her. *'I shall be a force for the public good.'*

Convinced it was her public duty to stand by him (you've got to admire his cheek), Mrs Lloyd George attended the trial at her husband's side. Lloyd George won the case, saved his career and got an apology and £1000 in damages. (His conscience must have been tender because he gave the money to a Welsh charity.)

THE BIG SHOWDOWN

When Lloyd's George's 'soak-the rich' budget reached them the Lords, who were all pretty well-fixed themselves, didn't care for it at all. In fact they totally rejected it.

This was breaking all the rules – up till now there'd been a gentleman's agreement that the Lords wouldn't interfere with money bills. But this bill, the Lords argued, wasn't just a money bill, it was downright socialism, dammit!

This was the final showdown between the (more or less) democratically elected House of Commons and the hereditary power of the House of Lords.

A SECOND ELECTION

Prime Minister Asquith decided to go to the country, and in 1910 there was a general election. Asquith wanted to pass a Parliament Bill, limiting the powers of the Lords. However, he didn't get the support he'd hoped for and the Liberals ended up with fewer seats than before. Now they were dependent on the support of the Irish and Socialist members to get a majority.

At this point King Edward VII died, and there was a sort of truce. The new king, George V, tried to get Lords and Commons to agree on some kind of compromise. (It's interesting to see that even as recently as this the king was still a major force in parliamentary politics.) But the king's attempt failed. Asquith dissolved Parliament and called another general election.

It was a draw – the Liberals and Conservatives got 272 seats each! However, with the help of his Irish and Socialist allies, Asquith was able to form a government. This time he had the rather reluctant support of the new king. If the Lords turned down the Parliament Bill, the king promised to create enough new Liberal peers to swamp the Lords. As had happened before, the mere threat

GEORGE V THREATENED TO CREATE ENOUGH NEW PEERS TO SWAMP THE LORDS

was enough. Horrified at the thought of having the place packed with johnny-come-lately peers, the Lords backed down, and the Parliament Bill was passed by both Commons and Lords in 1911.

THE COMMONS RULE – AT LAST!

The Parliament Bill made a number of important changes. The most important specifically concerned money bills – as opposed to other kinds of legislation. Money bills, once passed by the Commons, could be delayed by the Lords for one month – but no longer. (Whether a bill was a 'money bill' or not was to be decided *not* by the Lords but by the Speaker of the House of Commons.) All other bills were to become law if passed by the Commons in three consecutive sessions, which meant an effective delay of about two years.

Time between elections was cut down from seven to five years. The struggle between Parliament and Crown had been won by Parliament long ago. Now the Commons were victorious over the Lords. At last Britain was a truly democratic country. Or was it? One large group of British citizens was far from satisfied.

VOTES FOR WOMEN

The question of female suffrage (Votes for Women) had been around for quite some time. Way back in 1870 Queen Victoria said she was *'most anxious to enlist anyone who can speak or write to join in checking this mad wicked folly of "Women's Rights" with all its attendant horrors'*. (She must have had a premonition about Maggie Thatcher!)

With or without royal approval the campaign went ahead. In 1903 the Women's Social and Political Union, led by Mrs Emmeline Pankhurst, was formed. There was nothing weak and

WOMEN STILL DIDN'T HAVE THE VOTE

womanly about it either. Soon its militant members, known as suffragettes, were holding mass meetings, chaining themselves to the railings outside Parliament and heckling MPs. Militant protests reached a tragic climax in 1913 when a suffragette threw herself under the king's horse in the Derby and was killed.

EVERYBODY OUT!

The workers weren't too happy either, even though most of them had votes by now. Wages weren't keeping up with inflation (another all-too-familiar story). There were strikes by dock-workers, railwaymen and miners. Troops were called in and two miners were killed at Tonypandy in 1910.

In 1911 a national railway strike paralysed the country, and there was another massive miners' strike the following year. (So much for the good old days!)

However the struggles of workers and suffragettes were soon to be overshadowed by an even greater dispute, this time on an international scale.

THE FIRST WORLD WAR

By 1914 Europe was in a confused and stormy state. The Continent was a hotbed of old enmities and unresolved grudges. Everyone was worried about the growing power of Germany. Russia made an alliance with France, and so did Britain. The Germans felt everyone was ganging up on them and made an alliance with what was then Austria-Hungary.

In 1914 a Serbian student assassinated the Austrian Archduke Franz Ferdinand at Sarajevo, and this provided the trigger for World War I. This massive conflict involved Britain, France, Belgium, Russia, Denmark, Holland and Italy, and eventually America (the Allies) on one side, with Germany and Austria-Hungary on the other.

LLOYD GEORGE TAKES OVER

As often happens in war-time what is called a coalition government was formed. This means that all parties agree to work together during the crisis.

The coalition was led at first by Asquith. Things didn't go too well for the Allies in the first couple of years of the war, and in Britain it was Asquith who got the blame. In 1916 Lloyd George staged a cunning coup, ousting his own leader, and splitting the Liberal party in the process. As one of his cabinet colleagues observed, *'Lloyd George cares nothing for precedents and knows no principles, but he has fire in his belly and that is what we want.'*

Lloyd George was charismatic, cunning, ruthless and, as we've already seen, completely unscrupulous – all excellent qualities for a war-time leader. He carried on the war effort with great vigour, organising a smaller and more efficient war cabinet and taking firm control of the country's economy.

WINSTON'S UPS AND DOWNS

Another maverick politician rose to prominence in the First World War. Winston Churchill became First Lord of the Admiralty. Unfortunately a daring plan to attack Turkey, Germany's ally, proved a disaster; the Gallipoli campaign was an utter failure. Although Churchill had backed the plan, its failure wasn't really his fault. The plan was badly carried out and the attack insufficiently supported. But Churchill, unlike some of today's politicians, believed in accepting responsibility. He resigned, rejoined his old regiment as a Major and went to the front. Although a middle-aged man by now, he served in the thick of the fighting, winning promotion to Lieutenant-Colonel. But Churchill was too valuable to lose and by 1917 he was back in the Government as Minister of Munitions, working like a demon to get shells and ammunition to the troops.

The war ground on. The Americans joined the Allies and the Russians dropped out, preoccupied with their own Communist revolution. After four long and bloody years and the loss of millions of young lives the war finally came to an end with the Allies victorious.

VOTES FOR WOMEN – AND MEN TOO!

Women had done a magnificent job in the war, and not only in their traditional role as nurses. With so many men called up to fight, women took their place in shops, offices and factories all over the country, carrying out what were previously believed to be men's jobs. Women's sections of the armed forces were formed. After this, no one could call women helpless and impractical any more. Opposition to female suffrage largely disappeared. The men were still a bit cautious though. The vote was given to women over 30 who occupied, or whose husbands occupied, premises with a rental value of over £5.

Women were at last allowed to become MPs. In 1919 the Conservative Nancy Astor, Lady Astor actually, became the first woman to sit in the House of Commons, where she remained until 1945.

Quite a few more men got the vote as well. Property-owning qualifications were abolished. To vote you just had to be over 21 and to have lived in one place for six months.

All this doubled the number of people entitled to vote. The number of MPs in the house went up to 707.

SHUFFLING THE PARTY CARDS

With all these new voters it was time for another election. Lloyd George was seen as 'the man who'd won the war' – which was just what the wily Welsh wizard was banking on.

In the 1918 election his coalition government (Conservatives and Lloyd George Liberals) scored a landslide victory.

The rest of the Liberals, led by Asquith, got only 28 seats. The new Labour Party, however, got 59 seats. From now on Labour became the official opposition. The divided Liberals were never to form a government again.

PERILS OF PEACE

Everyone was looking forward to peace and prosperity, and the returning soldiers were promised *a land fit for heroes*. But there were lots of problems ahead.

At the victory peace conference at Versailles, Lloyd George, against his own political instincts, gave way to those who wanted to impose a harsh settlement on the beaten Germany. 'Make Germany pay' was a popular policy with the public and L-G went along with it. As he had suspected, it was a bad move. Post-war Germany eventually collapsed in chaos, and the end of the First World War planted the seeds of the second.

BOOM AND BUST

L-G's new government got off to a good start. 1919 and 1920 were boom years, marked by wage increases and rising inflation. But towards the end of 1921 the boom suddenly ended. Prices and wages fell and unemployment started rising, reaching two million by 1929. The Government tried to ease things by subsidising housing, and by extending unemployment insurance.

IRELAND AGAIN

The Irish problem refused to go away. The main trouble was that if the British were divided about Home Rule so were the Irish. The largely Catholic South wanted independence, the largely-Protestant North wanted to stay part of Britain. Both sides were prepared to fight for their beliefs.

In the 1918 election the Republican Sinn Fein party won most of the Irish seats, refused to go to Westminster and declared Ireland's independence. Britain tried to suppress the rebels and what has been called an undeclared war broke out.

Determined to end the bloodshed, Lloyd George managed to fix up a compromise. The 1921 agreement set up the Irish Free State giving Ulster, the mainly Protestant part, the right to withdraw, which it promptly did.

The compromise worked for a time, but it was only a patched-up solution. The problems of Ireland remain unsettled – as can be seen from the headlines almost every day!

AT THE TIME OF PARTITION THERE WERE 707 MPS IN A BUILDING DESIGNED FOR ONLY 650

GETS MY VOTE

IF WE GIVE THE IRISH HOME RULE, WE'LL LOSE 45 MPs

LLOYD GEORGE COMES A CROPPER

To add to L-G's troubles, his political enemies hadn't forgiven him. The Tory back-benchers – the ones who hadn't got jobs in the coalition – wanted to get back to the old party system. They'd never trusted L-G, fearing that he would divide the Conservatives just as he had the Liberals.

Brilliant politician that he was, Lloyd George was never really trusted and he never had the support of a loyal party behind him. It was the cause of his eventual downfall. At the 1922 election Lloyd George's coalition was defeated – he never held office again. Poor old Winston Churchill actually lost his seat in Parliament. (Don't worry, he'll be back . . .)

FARMER BALDWIN

A Canadian-born Scottish MP called Bonar Law was briefly Prime Minister until forced to retire by ill-health.

He was followed by Stanley Baldwin, a solid, reliable, pipe-smoking type who was universally liked and trusted. Keen on agriculture, Baldwin was usually pictured smoking a pipe and thoughtfully contemplating his pigs – he was known as Farmer Baldwin.

After a long dose of the wild Welsh wizard Lloyd George, the country was in the mood for someone safe, reliable and perhaps even a bit dull. (The Thatcher to Major syndrome maybe?) Nevertheless, Baldwin was a strong Parliamentary orator, who could turn a fine phrase when needed. In a later dispute with newspaper owners Beaverbrook and Rothermere he thundered, *'What the proprietorship of these papers is aiming at is power, and power without responsibility – the prerogative of the harlot throughout the ages.'*

FREE TRADE OR TARIFFS

By now the biggest difference between Liberals and Conservatives was that Liberals believed in Free Trade, while the Conservatives wanted to impose protective tariffs (taxes) on foreign goods. In 1922 Baldwin called a surprise election, hoping to win support for protective tariffs. Unfortunately for him the Conservatives lost 90 seats, Labour won an extra 50 and the Liberals, with 168, held the balance of power.

Asquith, the Liberal leader, refused to make an alliance with the Conservatives, preferring to back Labour instead. Baldwin resigned and in 1924, Britain had its first Labour Government.

LABOUR'S FIRST ATTEMPT

The Prime Minister was Ramsey Macdonald, a self-made Scot who had begun life as a journalist. As an MP he had opposed the war and a scandal sheet called 'John Bull' had demanded that he be *'Taken to the Tower and Shot at Dawn!'*

RAMSEY MACDONALD
"....THE GIFT OF COMPRESSING THE LARGEST AMOUNT OF WORDS INTO THE SMALLEST AMOUNT OF THOUGHT"

CHURCHILL

In true tabloid style, 'John Bull' later published an article revealing that Macdonald was the illegitimate son of a Scottish serving-girl. As well as stirring up scandal the story caused Macdonald great distress, but his career survived. He rose to become leader of the Labour Party and eventually Prime Minister. Ramsey Macdonald's inexperienced government had little success in tackling the country's economic problems, now in full swing. The new Labour Government couldn't even introduce any really socialist measures, since it was dependent on Liberal support. When Labour tried to recognise the new Communist regime in Russia, the Liberals withdrew their backing. The first Labour Government fell after less than a year in power.

BACK TO THE TORIES

The Conservatives won the next election with a handsome majority and the pipe-puffing Baldwin returned as PM.

By now Winston Churchill was back in Parliament, having joined, or rather re-joined, the Conservative Party. In 1925, much to Winston's astonishment and delight, Baldwin offered him a top Government job. *'When he said "Will you be Chancellor of the Exchequer" I was astonished . . . I should have liked to have answered "Will a bloody duck swim?" but as it was an important and formal conversation I replied, "This fulfils my ambition . . . I shall be delighted to serve you in this splendid Office."'*

THE GENERAL STRIKE

Then as now the coal miners were in a bad way. Their wages had dropped below the cost of living, the government planned to end the coal subsidy, and the mine owners, kind-hearted as ever, wanted to cut the miners' wages even further. The miners decided to strike – and the Trades Union Council called on all its members to strike in sympathy.

In 1926 Britain had its first-ever General Strike. Railways, buses, docks, iron and steel and chemical workers and many more all came out in support. It was a very British event though, with little violence and no real desire for revolution. The middle classes treated the whole thing as a sort of game, joining in to drive trains and buses and keep essential services running. The Government brought in troops. After 12 days the TUC called off the strike.

REPRESSION AND REFORM

Although the strikers had simply wanted a fair deal, the panicky Government felt the country had narrowly escaped a bloody revolution with a capitalist dangling from every lamp-post. As soon as the strike was over, Baldwin made all general strikes illegal. He also made it an offence for trade unions to use their members' subscriptions for political purposes – unless requested to do so in writing. Union membership fell by almost half. Apart from this bit of union bashing, little was done to solve the problems that had caused the strike in the first place. However the Government did help with the building of new houses. It also extended old age pensions and relief benefits and reformed the Poor Law. And in 1928 women were at last given the right to vote on the same terms as men.

LABOUR'S SECOND CHANCE

Baldwin's slogan for the 1929 election was 'safety first' but the voters weren't convinced. For the first time Labour actually won an election outright, by a narrow majority. Ramsey Macdonald became Prime Minister again – just as the Great Depression began. (Talk about bad timing . . .)

As depression moved across from America, things went from bad to worse. Macdonald proved an ineffective leader, unable to control his Cabinet or his party, failing to come up with anything new to solve the crisis. In 1931 a Parliamentary Committee warned of an approaching financial crash. Macdonald proposed to cut Government spending, including pensions and relief benefits. His Cabinet refused to accept the cuts and Macdonald resigned.

MACDONALD CRACKS UP

King George V persuaded Macdonald to head a Coalition Government, a mixture of Labour, Conservatives and Liberals. Free Trade was abandoned and protective tariffs were brought in for British and Commonwealth goods. Opposed to these measures, some Liberal and Labour ministers left the Government, which ended up as a mainly Conservative coalition – under a Labour Prime Minister!

By this time Macdonald, who seemed to have lost interest in Labour policies, was closer to the Conservatives. Much of the Labour party regarded him as a traitor. Moreover Macdonald was starting to crack up. His health was giving way under the strain. He began suffering from insomnia and from delusions, convinced that someone was going to shoot him from the visitors' gallery. Question Time was a torment and his speeches in Parliament became confused and sometimes almost meaningless. *'Trying to get something clear in my head for House of Commons tomorrow,'* he wrote in his diary, adding sadly, *'Cannot be done.'*

Crossing party lines he fell madly in love with a famous Tory hostess, the Marchioness of Londonderry, sending her passionate, if somewhat confused, love-letters. *'My Dear, you were very beautiful and I loved you . . . the dress, dazzling in brilliance and glorious in colour and line was you, and you were the dress . . .'*

In 1935 he resigned on grounds of ill health. That cuddly old Conservative Baldwin became Prime Minister for the third time.

BALDWIN'S COALITION

The country was glad to have Baldwin back and his coalition got a comfortable 428 seats at the next election. The Labour Party upped its seats to 154 and Clement Attlee became its new leader.

A NEW KING

The much-loved George V died in 1936. He was succeeded by his eldest son, who became King Edward VIII.

As the handsome, fair-haired, charming Prince of Wales he had been an enormously popular figure. Unfortunately, he wanted to marry a slim dark American lady called Wallis Simpson, who was already married to her second husband. When the Prince became King of Britain, and the lady became divorced for the second time, and so free to marry, things started to get tricky. The story began to leak out, first, as always in the foreign press, and then in Britain. School children began singing a new version of a popular Christmas Carol: *'Hark the Herald Angels sing*
Mrs Simpson's pinched our King!'

CONSTITUTIONAL CRISIS

Once the story became public knowledge there was a storm of comment and concern. Everyone had their say, politicians, newspaper proprietors, bishops, commonwealth prime ministers. It fell to Stanley Baldwin, the Prime Minister, to make the king accept the truth. Neither Parliament nor public would accept a twice-divorced woman as Queen of Britain. If the king insisted on marrying Mrs Simpson he would have to abdicate – which, eventually, he did. Baldwin handled the whole thing with masterly tact, gathering support from all parties. The Abdication Bill was passed by 403 votes to 5.

ANOTHER NEW KING

The ex-king, now Duke of Windsor, went off to a life of well-heeled exile, and his brother, the Duke of York, became King

George VI. Shy and stammering, always in the shadow of his more popular brother, the Duke had never expected to become king. Nor had his young wife, now our much-loved Queen Mother, ever thought that she would be queen. Luckily, both rose to their new roles magnificently. There were dark times ahead.

AND A NEW PM

Stanley Baldwin retired, pipe and all, in 1937, and was succeeded by another Conservative, Neville Chamberlain. A former Lord Mayor of Birmingham, he was the son of Joseph Chamberlain, a leading Liberal politician.

Lloyd George, who didn't think much of him, said he would probably have made *'a competent town clerk of Birmingham in a lean year'*. An upright gentlemanly chap with a rolled umbrella, Neville Chamberlain was hard-working, conscientious, and experienced in municipal administration and home affairs. Unfortunately for him, most of the approaching problems were coming from abroad.

NEVILLE'S TROUBLES

From the chaos of post-war Germany there had emerged a sinister new force, the National Socialist, or Nazi, Party, led by a hypnotically powerful orator called Adolf Hitler. With hindsight, three things about Adolf are pretty clear. He was a thoroughly nasty piece of work, he was as mad as a hatter and he was hell-bent on eventual war. Unfortunately not everyone realised this at the time. Winston Churchill had been thundering out warnings about Germany for years, but since he was a notorious eccentric and maverick no one took any notice of him.

The British public was still scarred by the memory of the terrible slaughter of World War I, which had ended less than 20 years ago. Most people and most politicians were against re-armament and keen to avoid war at almost any cost.

DEALS WITH THE DEVIL

Neville Chamberlain, a reasonable man himself, made the mistake of assuming that Hitler was reasonable too. He thought Adolf's demands were negotiable. Give him what he wanted and everyone could relax. He didn't realise that what Hitler wanted was everything.

Hitler started off by annexing neighbouring Austria in 1938. Britain made only a token protest. Hitler's next demand was for Sudetenland, a territory long disputed with Czechoslovakia. Soon afterwards Chamberlain met with Hitler at his Berchtesgaden headquarters, together with Mussolini, the Fascist dictator of Italy, and Daladier of France. Hitler insisted Sudetenland was his last territorial demand. Chamberlain believed him. Sudetenland was given to Hitler, who guaranteed to leave Czechoslovakia itself alone.

PEACE IN OUR TIME

Chamberlain came home to cheering crowds, waving a piece of paper, the famous Munich Agreement, signed by himself and Hitler. It meant, said Chamberlain, *'peace in our time'*. Some hopes. In 1939 Hitler broke the treaty and seized Czechoslovakia. A few months later he invaded Poland – a country with which both Britain and France had treaties of alliance. To Hitler's genuine astonishment, Britain and France declared war.

WINSTON'S FINEST HOUR

Hitler began the war with a string of successes, first in Poland, then in Denmark and Norway. A National Government was needed – but Labour refused to join a government led by Chamberlain. By now everyone realised that the honourable and old-fashioned Neville Chamberlain just wasn't the man to lead the country in war. But they knew a man who was . . .

In 1940 Chamberlain resigned, advising the king to ask Winston Churchill to form a government. One thing politics isn't is a young man's game. Churchill was 65 when he became Prime Minister. Many of his fellow politicians saw him as a maverick, an outsider, too eccentric and emotional to be really trusted. Some even saw him as a has-been, his career virtually over. Now he was leading the country in one of the most dangerous times in its history.

Churchill chose Labour's Clement Attlee as Deputy Prime Minister, and another Labour MP, Ernest Bevin, as Minister of Labour and National Service, keeping the vital post of Defence Minister for himself.

WORLD WAR II

Churchill led and inspired the nation during six long years of war. Even at the very beginning, when Hitler's armies rolled over Belgium, Holland and France, when the beaten remnant of the British army was evacuated from Dunkirk, Churchill never faltered. He inspired the country by the eloquence of his magnificent speeches in Parliament, promising them nothing at first but *'blood, toil, tears and sweat'*.

He found an immortal phrase for the young pilots who held off the German Air Force during the Battle of Britain: *'Never in the field of human conflict was so much owed by so many to so few.'* Churchill hurled defiance at the enemy when there was nothing else to throw. In perhaps his most famous speech he promised: *'We shall fight on the beaches . . . we shall fight in the fields and in the streets, we shall fight in the hills, we shall never surrender.'* As the House cheered Winston was heard to mutter, *'We'll have to beat the buggers about the head with bottles; that's all we've got!'* (With his legendary fondness for taking a drink or ten, he probably had a better supply of bottles than most people.)

WARTIME VICTORY

At the beginning of the war, Hitler's lightning conquest of most of the Continent left Britain facing Nazi Germany alone. As time went on Russia and America joined the struggle and the tide began to turn. In 1944 the Allied armies invaded German-occupied France. By 1945 the Germans had surrendered unconditionally, and Hitler had committed suicide in Berlin. In 1945 Churchill's prestige had never been higher. The war-time coalition was dissolved and there was a return to the party system. It was time for a general election. The Conservatives were confident. With Winston Churchill, *'the man who won the war'*, as their leader, victory in the 1945 election seemed certain.

In fact the result was a landslide – for their Labour opponents. Labour won 393 seats to the Conservatives' 189. The Liberals trailed way behind with only 11.

PEACETIME DEFEAT

The reason was a spirit of change in the British people. Returning soldiers, sailors and airmen, civilians who had suffered shortages and undergone the horrors of bombing at home, hadn't been fighting to put things back the way they were. They felt their efforts deserved a better, fairer world.

The Labour Party with its promise of social change appealed more to this mood than the Conservatives – who were still blamed by many for the policy of muddle and drift that had led into the war.

Strangely enough, Winston Churchill was as loved and revered as ever. The British electorate had simply decided that their great war-time leader wasn't the man they needed in peacetime.

ENTER UNCLE CLEM

Instead they chose the leader of the Labour Party, Clement Attlee, who became Prime Minister in the new Government. Unlike the burly and flamboyant Churchill, Attlee was unimpressive physically. Slight, bespectacled and balding, he looked rather like the typical 'little man' in a cartoon. But this mild appearance concealed a clever, tough-minded politician. (Like his great opponent Churchill, Attlee had fought in the First World War, surviving the worst of the fighting and emerging with the rank of Major.)

Winston Churchill, now demoted to Leader of the Opposition, generously admitted that Attlee had shown unexpected talents as a Prime Minister. *'Feed a bee on royal jelly,'* said Winston, *'and it becomes a Queen!'*

Attlee was the most unassuming of men, but success went to his head in at least one sense. On becoming Prime Minister he decided he ought to have a serious hat. His private secretary took him to Locks of St James Street, the poshest hatters in London. With an aristocratic black Homburg hat on his socialist head, Attlee set about revolutionising Britain.

ATTLEE
"FEED A BEE ON ROYAL JELLY AND IT WILL BECOME A QUEEN"

CHURCHILL

REFORMS GALORE

For the first time ever Labour had a clear overall majority and a mandate for reform. Used to taking orders in war-time, for once the British public was prepared to tackle post-war problems in the same disciplined way. Planning had worked during the war. Planning and increased control by the state were seen as the right way to manage the peace. The Labour Government embarked on an immense programme of state control called nationalisation. They started at the top with the Bank of England, and went on to nationalise the coal, gas and electricity industries. Air and transport services were nationalised as well.

THE LORDS' LAST STAND

Attempts to nationalise the iron and steel industry led to one last skirmish between Lords and Commons. The Lords were fiercely opposed to the bill – possibly because some of them owned iron and steel works. But the confident new Labour Government wasn't standing any nonsense. They simply amended the Parliament Act of 1911, reducing the Lords' power of delaying legislation from two years to one. The Iron and Steel Act was passed in 1949.

PROMISE AND PERFORMANCE

No doubt about it, nationalisation was a noble ideal. From now on, vital industries and services would be run not just for commercial profit but by, and for the benefit of, the people. At least, that was the idea. In practice it didn't always work out. For some strange reason, people with a job for life in a massive state-owned organisation didn't seem to work quite as hard as people running their own businesses and hoping to get rich on the proceeds.

THE NATIONAL HEALTH

One Labour idea that really was worthwhile was the provision of free medical care for everyone. Attlee's Health Minister was Aneurin Bevan, known as Nye, a Welsh orator in the Lloyd George tradition. His 1946 National Health Act made medical treatment, drugs, dentures, spectacles and hospitalisation completely free.

Financial considerations eventually interfered with this high ideal. A completely free service proved too expensive to run, and over the years charges were introduced for drug prescriptions, spectacles and dental treatment. But the important concept of free medical treatment – no doctor's bills – remains to this day.

WELFARE STATE

Over a million homes had been destroyed in the wartime bombing and a crash programme of house building got under way. Other reforms in what became known as the Welfare State included the National Insurance Act of 1946, which increased benefits in old age and sickness, and the National Assistance Act of 1948, which replaced the old Poor Law.

The Tory establishment reeled under the impact of all this left-wing legislation and made dire prophecies about a Russian-style Communist dictatorship – though the mild-mannered pipe-smoking Clem Attlee made an unlikely tyrant.

POST-WAR BLUES

Despite all its good works, the post-war Government was losing popularity. After winning the war, the British people had expected things to get better at once – but they didn't. The country was almost bankrupted by war and recovery was slow. Food was still rationed after the war – it took until 1954 to get rid of rationing altogether. Bread rationing actually *began* when the war was over. Goods of all kinds, especially luxury ones, were in short supply.

Moreover, the new welfare state had to be paid for and Labour was quite prepared to 'soak the rich'. Income tax in the higher brackets rose to a punishing 88%.

ELECTIONS AGAIN

Confident in his government's record of reform, Attlee went into the 1950 election, announcing plans for still more nationalisation.

The Conservatives offered less state control, not more, and an end to nationalisation – though they cunningly promised to maintain the Health Service and the rest of the welfare state.

The public must have been listening – the election reduced Labour's majority to only six seats.

FESTIVAL TIME

The Government tried to cheer everyone up with the 1951 Festival of Britain, marking the centenary of the Great Exhibition of 1851. Colourful pavilions were set up on the South Bank of the Thames – though the British climate being what it is, it rained most of the time. Problems kept raining down on Attlee's government. The Korean War broke out and the expense of re-armament meant higher taxes. Ernest Bevin died and Nye Bevan and Harold Wilson, both on the left of the party, resigned because they disagreed with Attlee's foreign policy. In a desperate gamble, Attlee called another election in late 1951.

This time the Tories won by a narrow margin – 321 seats to 295.

THE TORIES RETURN

At the fine old age of 77, Winston Churchill became Prime Minister for the second time. Although still in fine robust form, he was beginning to suffer from deafness and, as an experiment, microphones and loudspeakers were installed around the Cabinet table. The experiment came to a sudden end when a taxi-driver called at No 10 and complained that he'd picked up the entire Cabinet meeting on his taxi radio driving down Whitehall.

The handsome and elegant Anthony Eden, seen as Churchill's eventual successor, became Foreign Secretary. The talented Rab Butler became Chancellor of the Exchequer.

True to their word the Tories hung on to the popular parts of

Labour's achievements, the National Health Service and the welfare state, although they immediately de-nationalised iron and steel. Just as Labour had got the blame for post-war problems, the Tories got the credit for the coming recovery.

NEW ELIZABETHANS

King George VI died in 1952 and his daughter Queen Elizabeth II, the present queen, came to the throne. People started talking about a New Elizabethan age of peace and prosperity. Things were looking better than at any time since the war. World economic conditions improved, production rose and so did the standard of living. In the coming years wages rose by as much as 50 per cent. It was the time of conspicuous consumption – sales and production rose steadily. It was too good to last – and it didn't.

Winston Churchill retired in 1955, still going strong at 81. He was followed, as expected, by Anthony Eden who called an immediate election, increasing the Tory majority to 60.

ENTER THE WALRUS

Eden's place as Chancellor of the Exchequer was taken over by Harold Macmillan, an old-style Tory who masked a keen political brain beneath his old-world charm. His heavy eyelids and drooping moustache earned him the nickname of 'The Walrus'.

Macmillan was a publisher and something of an intellectual. As a young officer in the First World War, he had consoled himself by reading the Greek Classics amidst the blood and bullets of the trenches.

As Chancellor, Macmillan found himself faced with problems over the balance of payments, growing inflation and declining production.

EDEN'S DOWNFALL

The handsome Anthony Eden had waited for so long to become Prime Minister that he seemed worn out by the time he got the job. He was scuppered by the Suez Crisis when Britain, combining with France to seize the Suez Canal, was made to back down by the USA. Suddenly Britain wasn't top nation any more. Eden resigned because of ill-health and Macmillan became PM.

UNCLE MAC

Macmillan was a Tory moderate with a genuine concern for the welfare of ordinary people. He hated unemployment, and fought hard for full employment throughout his career.

Attlee once described him as *'the most radical man I've known in politics. If it hadn't been for the war he'd have joined the Labour Party. If that had happened, Macmillan would have been Labour's Prime Minister, not me.'*

A colourful elegant figure, Macmillan was nicknamed 'Mac' or even 'SuperMac' by the cartoonists. He was popular with the electorate, who loved his Edwardian appearance and manners. Unlike the over-conscientious Eden who'd worked himself into a breakdown, the unflappable Mac believed in taking things calmly. In a later interview he said, *'I enjoyed being Prime Minister because I found it the most relaxed of all the offices I held. I didn't work so hard . . . Oh, you had the Cabinet to run and all that. I found I read a lot of books and so on. It's a great mistake to get yourself into a state of nervous excitement all the time . . . nobody should overdo it, you know. You should read Jane Austen and then you'll feel better.'*

Holding the party together, Macmillan presided over some of the most prosperous of Britain's post-war years. He fought the 1959 election on the slogan: *'You never had it so good!'* The voters must have believed him – they increased the Tory majority to over 100.

UNLUCKY LABOUR

The Labour Party meanwhile were fighting each other instead of the Tories. When Attlee retired, there was a bitter struggle for the premiership. The main contenders were Aneurin Bevan from the old working-class Labour left and Hugh Gaitskell, a university lecturer, who represented the more moderate middle-class elements in the party.

Gaitskell won, becoming party leader in 1955. (Formerly Chancellor of the Exchequer, Gaitskell had once observed, *'Sometimes Cabinet meetings horrify me because of the amount of rubbish talked by some Ministers . . .'*)

Gaitskell's victory over Bevan marked a change in party style that eventually led to such leaders as Neil Kinnock and John Smith. Some people said the Labour Party was modernising, becoming a party of government. Others, on the far left, said it was selling out and losing its soul.

On Gaitskell's death in 1963, Harold Wilson, formerly a lecturer in economics at Oxford, followed Gaitskell as party leader.

MIDDLE OF THE ROAD

It's interesting to note that by now the policies of the two parties weren't really all that different. Labour was less keen on nationalising everything in sight, and its links with the trade unions were weakening.

The Tories had accepted most of Labour's 'welfare state' policies, and accepted the need for at least some Government control of the economy.

Politics became less a matter of policy and more one of personalities. It didn't make the contest any less bitter.

MAC THE KNIFE

Things got tougher for Mac right after his victory in the 1959 election. The boom was over and the balance of payments was in a bad way.

One member of the Cabinet who didn't approve of Mac's easy-going ways was the stern and puritan Enoch Powell, at that time Minister of Health. Lord Home tells of coming into the Cabinet Room one day to find the Cabinet Secretary changing round all the places. Home asked if there had been a re-shuffle.

'Oh no,' said the secretary, *'it's nothing like that. The Prime Minister cannot stand Enoch Powell's steely and accusing eye looking at him across the table any more, and I've had to move him down the side.'*

But Mac could be tough when he had to be. Desperate to get the economy right, he changed Chancellors three times. He sacked and re-shuffled so many ministers he became known as 'Mac the Knife'

MAC THE KNIFE
"GREATER LOVE HATH NO MAN, THAT HE LAY DOWN HIS FRIENDS FOR HIS LIFE"

THORPE

– but nothing seemed to work.

Then came Profumo.

THE PROFUMO SCANDAL

John Profumo, Macmillan's Secretary for War, was by no means the first minister to have a bit on the side.

Unfortunately the young lady he chose, a certain Christine Keeler, was also good friends with a certain Captain Ivanov, a Naval attaché at the Russian Embassy.

When the news broke there was a big juicy scandal involving nude bathing in a country house swimming-pool, another young lady called Mandy Rice-Davies, an osteopath called Stephen Ward who conveniently committed suicide, and quite a few names in top political and social circles.

It's doubtful if there was any real security risk – Ivanov seems to have been more of a good-time Charlie than a Russian master-spy. But Profumo made the mistake of lying to the House of Commons about his association with Christine Keeler – an unforgivable sin for an MP. When the truth came out he was forced to resign.

GOODBYE MAC

Worn out and fed up with the whole sordid business, Macmillan too resigned in 1963. There were plenty of candidates for his job, but not one of them could win a clear majority in the party. So Mac chose his own successor, the Foreign Secretary, Lord Home. For some inscrutable Tory reason, R A Butler, called by many 'the best Prime Minister we never had', was passed over. One Tory MP said Macmillan was always determined that Butler should never succeed him – exactly why, we'll probably never know.

ENTER ALEC

Renouncing his title so that he could sit in the Commons, Lord Home turned into Sir Alec Douglas-Home. The new PM was a tall, thin, rather Bertie Woosterish type with an incredibly posh accent.

ALEC DOUGLAS-HOME
"THOSE SILLY BAGS BEHIND A
SHOT-GUN, BLOWING OFF ON
GROUSE MOORS AND COUNTING
WITH MATCHSTICKS, ARE ALL
REMINISCENT OF A PAST AGE AND
MAKE A POOR SHOWING FOR THE
TORIES"

NABARRO

He later admitted, *'I never understood a word about economics,'* and is famous for confessing that even his arithmetic was shaky – he had to work out difficult sums by using matches as counters. Despite these handicaps, Sir Alec was an intelligent and able politician, and made a highly-competent Prime Minister.

If he's not as well remembered as he might be, it's perhaps because, like Clement Attlee before him, he was a genuinely shy and modest man. Home must have been one of the last Prime Ministers actually to *avoid* publicity.

He admits to underestimating the growing power of television. *'I was bored by the whole of presentation as far as television was concerned because I think television is bound to be superficial . . . Harold Wilson convinced me I was wrong because he trained himself very, very well to be a pretty good television performer, and I think it's necessary for the Prime Minister.'* After 13 years of the Tories – 13 years of Tory misrule as Labour put it – some at least of the electorate were feeling it was time for a change . . .

The election of 1964 put Labour in power – with a lead of just four seats.

WILSON TAKES OVER

Although handicapped by his tiny majority, Wilson made a good job of his first administration, moving the party firmly towards the centre.

His personality helped – Harold Wilson was always well aware of the importance of a politician's public image. Unlike the rather wispy Douglas-Home, Wilson was a solid, stocky-looking man, reassuringly silver-haired with an amiably froggy face. Despite his Oxford background, he spoke in a reassuringly down-to-earth

WILSON
ALL THROUGH HIS PREMIERSHIP, HE WAS PARANOID THAT MI5 WAS
BUGGING HIM - AS IT TURNED OUT, HE WAS RIGHT

Yorkshire accent. And he smoked a pipe – the best possible way for a politician to project solid dependability. Actually, Wilson was said to prefer a good cigar to a pipe – but only in private. Big cigars have far too much of a Tory image for a socialist Prime Minister. Perhaps it's not surprising that amongst his parliamentary colleagues, Harold Wilson had a reputation for extraordinary deviousness and cunning . . .

In 1965 Wilson called another election, determined to increase the slender Labour lead. He promised to transform the country with 'the white heat of technology'. The gamble was successful, raising the Labour lead to a comfortable 90 seats.

During his time in power, Wilson made good use of the still fairly new medium of television, reassuring the electorate with cosy fireside chats. In reality he was having little success in grappling with the old problems of rising inflation and low productivity. There was a plague of unofficial strikes – always tricky for a trade-union-backed Labour Government – and in 1967 the Government decided to devalue the pound. Wilson assured the electors that 'the pound in your pocket' was worth just as much. They didn't believe him.

One more important electoral change took place in 1969 – the voting age was lowered from 21 to 18. Hoping no doubt to pick up a few young voters, Wilson appeared on TV singing along with the Beatles.

SAILOR TED

Much had changed in the Tory Party meanwhile. Sir Alec Douglas-Home had decided to resign in favour of a younger man and Ted Heath became party leader. Heath, like Wilson, was a solid, stocky chap, with a red face, white hair and bright blue eyes. Passionately fond of yachting, he was affectionately known as Sailor Ted. He was a keen musician too, and loved conducting orchestras and choirs.

Heath was hard-working and competent, with a particular interest in the administrative machinery of government. At one time he had considered becoming a permanent civil servant. Indeed, he often seemed happier in the company of permanent secretaries and other senior civil servants than in that of his cabinet colleagues. As a personality, Heath was the strong silent type, so much so that he sometimes appeared stolid and humourless. The cunning, quick-thinking Wilson could usually talk rings round him in the House. All the same, Ted's turn was coming . . .

SAILOR TED

HELLO SAILOR

With Labour ahead in the public opinion polls – another important new factor in politics – Wilson called another election in 1970. But, as we've since learned, polls can be deceptive. Sailor Heath achieved a surprise success. The Conservatives won the election by 330 seats to 287 – the poor old Liberals only got 6.

Ted started off with massive tax cuts – always a popular move. Strongly pro-European, he led Britain's move into the Common Market. Turned down twice before, largely because of the opposition of France's De Gaulle, Britain finally became a member in 1973 – the year that De Gaulle passed away.

Ted's real troubles were caused by the trade unions who were getting increasingly stroppy. When strikes reached an all-time high, the Tories tried to tame the unions with the 1971 Industrial Relations Act which outlawed the 'closed shop' – compulsory union membership.

But things just got worse. In 1973 the mineworkers demanded a massive 30 per cent wage increase. Heath declared a state of emergency and put the country on a three-day working week. He offered the miners a 15 per cent rise. They refused and went on a nationwide strike. Heath called a general election, fighting it on the slogan 'Who Governs Britain?'

WILSON AGAIN

The election results were inconclusive with Labour winning 311 seats, Conservatives 296, Liberals 14 and other (very) small parties 20. No one had a clear majority over everyone else. Heath tried to form a Conservative-Liberal pact. The Liberals wouldn't play. So the queen called upon Harold Wilson, who formed the first minority Government since 1929.

Wilson settled the miners' strike by giving in to the miners, and got rid of the Industrial Relations Act. Then he called another election. He won, with a majority of just three seats. It seemed the British electorate just couldn't make up its mind . . .

A NEW PM

British politics went on its erratic way, the story twisting and turning like an out-of-control soap opera. In 1976 Wilson mysteriously resigned. Was it because Parliament had turned down his plans to cut expenditure? Or was it because, as some later alleged, maverick MI5 officers were trying to prove he was really a Russian spy? Who knows? It was getting hard to keep track of the plot.

Wilson was followed by the easy-going avuncular figure of Jim Callaghan, a far more traditionally-minded old-style Labour politician with a solid working-class and trade union background. He believed that *'The fortunes of the trade unions and of the Labour Party cannot be separated.'* (A journalist christened Callaghan, *'The Keeper of the Cloth Cap'*.)

Callaghan's determined cheerfulness earned him the nickname of *'Sunny Jim'*.

In 1977 Callaghan boosted his majority by forming a pact with the Liberals. For three years he was able to follow a stable anti-inflation policy, and things seemed to be looking up.

TORY REVIVAL

The Tory Party is merciless towards failure and after the defeat of 1974 Sailor Ted was swiftly heaved overboard.

Still with us in Parliament, he sits on the back benches, looking down on the Prime Ministers who have followed him with what one commentator calls *'an air of stupendous disapproval'*!

The surprise winner in the ballot for party leader was Margaret Hilda Thatcher, who led the Conservatives into the next election. A strikingly forceful female with a corrugated-iron hairstyle and a voice that could shatter glass, she had earlier been nicknamed *'Margaret Thatcher, milk snatcher'* when she oversaw the end of free school milk. Now she was to become the first woman to lead a major party in Europe or in America. (Not that she did a lot for the feminist cause. She was later referred to as the Iron Lady – or *'the best man in the House'*.) Maggie, as she was known, not always affectionately, was to be the dominant figure in British politics for many years.

NO CONFIDENCE FOR CALLAGHAN

In 1979 Callaghan's policy of wage restraint and inflation control suddenly exploded in a wave of strikes, the worst and most severe since 1926. Conservatives called it *'the winter of discontent'*.

Callaghan was suddenly confronted with a Labour Prime Minister's nightmare – a head-on clash with the trade unions. To fend off the strikes the Government had to agree to wage increases as high as 20 per cent.

CALLAGHAN
"CRISIS - WHAT CRISIS?"

In the Commons a motion of no confidence in the Government was passed by 311 votes to 310. That one vote mean another election.

MAGGIE WINS

Led by Mrs Thatcher, who became Europe's first female Prime Minister, the Conservatives won the election with a clear 43-seat majority. Sir Geoffrey Howe became Chancellor of the Exchequer, and Lord Carrington Foreign Secretary.

THATCHER
"ADDS THE DIPLOMACY OF ALF GARNETT TO
THE ECONOMICS OF ARTHUR DALEY"

HEALEY

Maggie swung into action straight away.

She cut taxes, again, as ever, a popular move.

She forced the trade unions to accept secret ballots to elect officials and to authorise strikes, and she banned secondary picketing – one union picketing in support of another.

Reversing Labour's policy of nationalisation, she began a privatisation programme, offering shares in British Aerospace.

THE PRICE OF SUCCESS

Government determination to hold down inflation and to cut expenditure was not without painful consequences. Inflation fell to 8 per cent but unemployment rose to over three million – the highest figure since the Great Depression of the '30s. The gap between rich and poor widened and there were riots in London, Liverpool and other cities. On the other hand productivity rose faster than in any other country in Europe.

Mrs Thatcher's insistence on freezing social service expenditure and increasing defence spending came near to causing revolt in her own Cabinet – but no one dared to speak out.

TEBBIT THE TERRIBLE

Maggie may have had her opponents – terrified into silence as they were – but she also had many loyal supporters. One of the most loyal was Norman Tebbit.

A self-made man from a modest suburban background, Tebbit qualified as an RAF pilot during National Service, and went on to be a pilot with BOAC. Involvement in BALPA, the pilots' union, led him on to politics and he entered Parliament in 1970 at the start of Ted Heath's government.

But it was when Maggie took over that Tebbit rose to fame. No public-school Tory wimp, Tebbit was exactly what the Conservatives needed – a tough street-fighter with a gift for fierce political debate. The usually mild Michael Foot, who had replaced Callaghan as Labour Party leader, was provoked into calling Tebbit *'a semi-house-trained polecat'*.

THE CHINGFORD SKINHEAD

Tebbit enjoyed intimidating the opposition, a task in which he was aided by fierce, skull-like features which gave him a rather frightening look – like Dracula on a bad day. Since his constituency was in Essex, he was also referred to as *'The Chingford Skinhead'*.

A Thatcherite to the core, Tebbit advised anyone who was unemployed to *'Get on your bike'* – and look for another job. He opposed the trade union principle of the closed shop, calling his opponents *'red fascists!'*

Tebbit entered the Cabinet as Employment Secretary in 1981 and became party Chairman in 1985.

When the IRA tried to blow up Mrs Thatcher during the Brighton conference in 1984, Norman Tebbit was badly injured in the blast. His wife was crippled for life.

Refusing to give up, Tebbit battled on. He fell out with Maggie over tactics in the 1987 election, when he unwisely showed her research which said she was seen as *'harsh and uncaring'*. In 1990 he supported Maggie's BBC-bashing with a typical piece of Tebbit oratory. *'The word "Conservative" is now used by the BBC as a portmanteau word of abuse for anyone whose political views differ from the insufferable, smug, sanctimonious, naive, guilt-ridden, wet, pink orthodoxy of that sunset home of that third-rate decade the 1960s.'* The old polecat could still snap. Tebbit stayed on to support the Tories in the 1992 election before retiring – leaving the Commons a duller, if politer and quieter, place.

SMOOTH CECIL

Another keen Thatcher supporter was Cecil Parkinson. Like Tebbit he had risen from the working classes, though you'd never have thought it to look at him. Smooth, elegant and handsome, Cecil Parkinson admitted to being attracted to strong women. Not surprisingly he and Maggie hit it off right away. He was her right-hand man during the Falklands War (see below) and he ran the 1983 election as party Chairman.

Like many another politician before him, Cecil Parkinson was brought down by scandal. He was a married man – and his secretary Sara Keays suddenly announced she was pregnant – and was *not* proposing to keep quiet about it. Even before the news became public, this cost poor Cecil Parkinson a top job. He had been destined for Foreign Secretary, but with a scandal coming up it was thought unwise to promote him to such a high-profile post. Once the news broke Maggie did her best to support him, but the scandal grew and grew until he had to resign from the Cabinet.

CECIL'S COMEBACK

After what turned out to be a fairly short time out in the cold, Parkinson, still a Thatcher favourite, made a come-back, firstly as Energy Secretary, later as Minister of Transport. Somehow luck seemed to have deserted him. He wasn't reckoned to be a great success in either post, and with the eventual departure of his beloved leader his once-promising career seems to be fading away . . .

A NEW PARTY

Meanwhile, what about the workers?

Under Michael Foot's leadership, the Labour Party was still divided in defeat. There was a continuing struggle between moderates and such left-wing militants as Tony Benn.

Four former Labour Cabinet members, Roy Jenkins, David Owen, William Rodgers and Shirley Williams, resigned to form a new centrist party, the Social Democrats or SDP, hoping to appeal to middle-of-the-road voters disenchanted with both Labour and Conservatives. The new party gained an impressive number of seats in by-elections, eventually achieving 28 MPs.

They later formed an alliance with David Steel's 12-strong Liberal Party.

THE FALKLANDS FACTOR

Things were beginning to look black for Maggie by 1982. Her tough policies had made her the most unpopular PM in the history of opinion polls.

Then she had a stroke of political luck. The even more unpopular military government of Argentina tried to raise its political profile by invading the Falkland Islands, a British possession long claimed by Argentina.

Maggie reacted with characteristic decision, sending off a naval task force and giving the United Nations an earful as well. After a brief but bloody campaign, British troops re-conquered the islands. *'Rejoice!'* said Maggie, and her popularity soared again.

The Labour Party seemed completely demoralised. Its 1983 election manifesto was described as *'the longest suicide note in history'* – by Gerald Kaufman, who was on their own side!

In the 1983 elections the Conservatives won 397 seats, Labour 209 and the new SDP-Liberal Alliance only 23.

It was the biggest landslide victory since Labour's win in 1945.

MAGGIE CARRIES ON

Justified by her victory, Maggie carried on with her policies. Twenty-nine formerly state-owned industries were privatised, and people were encouraged to invest in shares on the stock market.

Maggie also went on to confront the unions. When the Government planned to cut subsidies to the still-struggling coal industry, militant miners' leader Arthur Scargill ordered a strike. It dragged on for 11 weary months, causing great suffering to miners and their families. Maggie was unyielding – and she'd taken care that there were ample stocks of coal. The miners surrendered, going back to work with nothing to show for the strike.

It seemed that the trade unions were tamed at last. 1985 showed the lowest number of strikes for 50 years, and trade union membership has been falling year by year ever since 1979 . . .

ENTER KINNOCK

The Labour Party had been in opposition for so long now it was starting to look permanent. In a desperate attempt to buck themselves up they changed leaders once again, replacing the leftist Michael Foot with the more centrist Neil Kinnock, an eloquent (some said windy) Welshman in the Lloyd George tradition. Engaging and affable, Kinnock worked hard to pull things together, striving for a modern middle-of-the-road Labour Party, led by men in respectable dark suits. (So much for Keir Hardie's cloth cap and brass band . . .)

Likeable as he was, Kinnock knew how to be ruthless. He cracked down hard on the 'Loony Lefties' in the party, whom he saw as making the party unelectable.

Meanwhile the SDP-Liberal Alliance trundled on. After a surprisingly promising start its members were already squabbling amongst themselves. The Alliance was eventually to split up.

MAGGIE WINS AGAIN

Meanwhile the country was still enjoying a boom. Maggie's reputation grew steadily, not only at home but on the world stage. Seen as the kind of strong, confident leader the world needs, the 'Iron Lady' became immensely popular in America and on the Continent.

Maggie had been one of the first to welcome the liberalisation of Russia and to announce that we could *do business with Gorbachev*. In 1987, after a successful visit to Moscow, she called another election. Despite all Kinnock's best efforts, she scored the third Conservative win in a row, with a solid Tory majority of 105. This made her the first PM to do the hat-trick for 160 years.

After the election, Maggie persevered with her plan to make Britain *a property-owning democracy*. People were encouraged to buy shares, to start businesses and to buy their own homes – especially those living in council houses.

POLL TAX PROBLEMS

Suddenly Maggie ran into an unexpected setback. The 1988 Local Government Finance Act was intended to replace the old 'rates' – the local government tax paid by all property owners.

The plan was to substitute a 'poll tax' paid by everyone, property-owning or not, between the ages of 18 and 65. (Maggie is said to have bulldozed this scheme through her extremely unenthusiastic Cabinet.) The whole thing sounds fair enough in theory – but in practice it was a political time bomb. People saw the new law as being easy on the rich and hard on the poor. There was a storm of civil – and sometimes very uncivil – protest. Lots of people just flatly refused to pay and the courts became clogged up with poll tax cases. A 40,000-strong protest march in central London turned into a major riot.

IN OR OUT OF EUROPE?

Troubles never seem to come singly. Once a lady who could do no wrong, Maggie was suddenly under attack from many sides. Although she had supported the move into the Common Market, Maggie had never been a great enthusiast for it. She was very much against anything that might infringe on British sovereignty, and there was a general feeling that she was anti-Europe, dragging her feet whenever she could.

In 1990 at a summit meeting in Rome, everyone voted for a measure that would introduce a common European currency by the year 2000. Everyone but Maggie – she voted no . . . '*No, no and no!*' she cried later in the House of Commons.

Astonishingly, this marked the beginning of her downfall – which was to come about with amazing speed.

MAGGIE MUST GO

In reality, poll tax protests and European doubts were just symptoms of a larger discontent. The country was beginning to feel that 12 years of Maggie Thatcher were more than enough. By now a world recession was beginning to bite.

People who'd bought their own homes could no longer afford to pay the mortgage. Lots of those small businesses people had been encouraged to start were collapsing into bankruptcy. Crime statistics were rising all the time. Inflation was down but unemployment was way, way up. Hospital wards and even hospitals were closing. The rich might be getting richer but the poor were definitely getting poorer. Homeless people were living in cardboard boxes and for the first time in 100 years beggars became a common sight on the streets of London and other big cities.

Maggie had taken all the credit for the good times. Now she was getting most of the blame for the bad . . .

ATTACK OF A DEAD SHEEP

The first dagger between the shoulder-blades came from an unlikely source. Sir Geoffrey Howe, Maggie's Deputy Prime Minister, was a mild-mannered man. A Parliamentary colleague said that being attacked by Geoffrey Howe was like being savaged by a dead sheep. But if worms can turn, so can sheep.

Howe resigned, ostensibly over Maggie's 'no' vote in Rome. In a quietly deadly resignation speech he attacked Maggie's instinctive hostility to Europe, a place she seemed to think was *teeming with ill-intentioned persons*. He said that he had for too long remained silent when he should have spoken up – and so, he hinted, had many others.

Maggie's bossiness and her iron grip on her Cabinet were much resented. The golden-haired Michael Heseltine, popularly known as 'Tarzan', had already resigned. Now he mounted a challenge to her leadership. It failed, but only just.

One by one her Cabinet ministers told her the bad news. It was time for her to go. Rather than face defeat, Mrs Thatcher resigned.

THE NEW PM

There were three main contenders for her job.

One was the charismatic Heseltine, dynamic, colourful, even flashy but still something of an outsider.

The second, and perhaps the more likely, was the talented and popular Douglas Hurd, the Foreign Secretary but he was seen as being rather too patrician for the 'classless' society.

The race was won by the third candidate, the Chancellor of the Exchequer, that nice Mr Major.

THAT NICE MR. MAJOR

A MAJOR CHANGE

John Major was everything Maggie Thatcher was not. He was quiet where she was strident and he was reasonably pro-Europe. Grey-suited, bespectacled, supremely ordinary, he came from a modest but colourful background – his parents had been circus acrobats who had left show business to go into the garden gnome business and fallen on hard times.

After a shaky start, young Major got himself a good job in a bank and began a steady rise. He started in politics on Lambeth Council where he encountered Ken Livingstone. Although dedicated political opponents, Major and 'Red Ken' always got on well. Twenty years later they met again. *'You know me, Ken,'* said Major. *'I haven't changed. And one day I'll be able to do what I want.'*

MAJOR RISES

When Major first arrived in Parliament he was quietly and unobtrusively successful, serving for a time as a Whip, one of the Government officials who keep MPs in order.

One night Mrs Thatcher dined with the Whips' Office, and Major astonished everyone by telling her that her economic policies were not popular with the party. *'You astound me,'* said Mrs T frostily, and proceeded to deliver a severe verbal handbagging. But John Major stood his ground. *'Hang on,'* said Major. *'I'm telling you what the* party *think. That's* what *they think – whether it's acceptable or not.'* After dinner, Dennis Thatcher is said to have slapped Major on the back, saying, *'That will have done the old girl a lot of good. She loves an argument.'*

It certainly didn't seem to do John Major any harm. He became one of Mrs Thatcher's favourites, eventually entering her Cabinet as Chief Secretary to the Treasury in 1987. He scored a success in a difficult and often unpopular job, proving, as someone said, that you could be a Thatcherite and a nice person as well.

In 1989 there was a Cabinet re-shuffle. Mrs Thatcher had lost confidence in Geoffrey Howe her Foreign Secretary, feeling he had 'gone native' and was too soft on Europe. She replaced him with John Major. A few months later, Nigel Lawson, the Chancellor of the Exchequer, resigned, increasingly fed up with Maggie's interference. Before his Foreign Office seat had even had time to get warm, John Major took Lawson's place as Chancellor of the Exchequer. Finally, when it was clear she really had to go, Mrs Thatcher supported Major as her successor.

MAJOR TAKES CHARGE

Once he became PM, John Major lost no time in mending fences. He reduced the hated poll tax and announced it would soon be replaced. He promised Britain would be a full partner in Europe. And he prepared to lead the Conservatives into the next election.

A SURPRISE RESULT

Of course everyone knew he hadn't a chance. The recession was darkening into depression. After 12 years of government, the Tories must surely take the blame.

Neil Kinnock had united Labour, moved them away from the more unpopular socialist ideas and forged them into a credible party of government. The Labour Party was consistently doing well in the pre-election public opinion polls. It was only a matter of time before Kinnock became Prime Minister.

In April 1992 John Major called a general election – and won by a comfortable majority.

TO BE CONTINUED

Quite how he managed it is hard to say. Perhaps the truth is that even with the economy in depression the voters think the Tories have a better chance of sorting it out than do Labour.

Image is everything in politics these days and Kinnock, although much liked, never quite gained the electorate's confidence.

Neil Kinnock resigned as party leader straight after the election. Now solid, Scottish John Smith is carrying on his good work, confident Labour *must* win an election one day . . .

Just follow the next thrilling instalment in this Parliamentary saga.

You'll find it all in tomorrow's news . . .

Part Two

THE PALACE OF WESTMINSTER

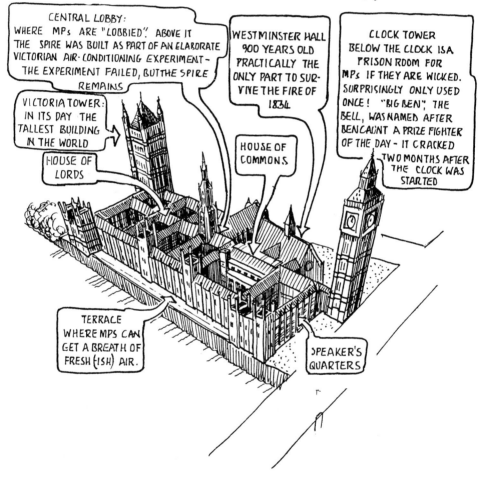

CENTRAL LOBBY:
WHERE MPs ARE "LOBBIED". ABOVE IT THE SPIRE WAS BUILT AS PART OF AN ELABORATE VICTORIAN AIR-CONDITIONING EXPERIMENT— THE EXPERIMENT FAILED, BUT THE SPIRE REMAINS

WESTMINSTER HALL 900 YEARS OLD PRACTICALLY THE ONLY PART TO SURVIVE THE FIRE OF 1834

CLOCK TOWER BELOW THE CLOCK IS A PRISON ROOM FOR MPs IF THEY ARE WICKED. SURPRISINGLY ONLY USED ONCE! "BIG BEN", THE BELL, WAS NAMED AFTER BEN CAUNT A PRIZE FIGHTER OF THE DAY — IT CRACKED TWO MONTHS AFTER THE CLOCK WAS STARTED

VICTORIA TOWER: IN ITS DAY THE TALLEST BUILDING IN THE WORLD

HOUSE OF LORDS

HOUSE OF COMMONS

TERRACE WHERE MPs CAN GET A BREATH OF FRESH (ISH) AIR.

SPEAKER'S QUARTERS

Part Two

PARLIAMENT TODAY

What does Parliament really mean today? Is it a collection of people, a place or an institution? As a matter of fact it's all three.

THE INSTITUTION

Parliament is the supreme governing body, the law-making authority of Great Britain.

Strictly speaking it consists of:

The House of Commons – elected.

The House of Lords – largely hereditary, but also including the Lords Spiritual (Bishops and Archbishops) and more recently Life Peers (and Peeresses).

The Monarch – the king, or as at present, the queen.

THE POWER OF PARLIAMENT

The fact that Great Britain has no written Constitution only increases Parliament's power. It can make – or un-make – any law. Once an Act of Parliament has been properly passed it cannot be challenged or disputed by any legal means.

THE LORDS

The House of Lords has 1189 members at the present time.

First (and holiest) there are the Lords Spiritual – two Archbishops and 24 Bishops.

Next come the Lords Temporal – 764 hereditary peers. Many of them are traditional landed gentry of the 'huntin' shootin' and fishin'' kind, affectionately known as 'backwoodsmen'. Not surprisingly, most of them are Conservatives in both senses of the word. Some hereditary peers never come to the House of Lords at all. (If absolutely everyone turned up there just wouldn't be room.) Others doze quietly through all the debates. Many make valuable and useful contributions.

The hereditary peers include a number of newly-created Lords, awarded a hereditary peerage by the Government. Ted Heath, when Prime Minister, decreed there should be no more hereditary peerages created. Maggie Thatcher, when she succeeded him, started handing them out again.

A retiring Prime Minister or Minister nearly always goes to the Lords either as a hereditary or a life peer. Labour PM Clement Attlee ended up as an Earl, as did Conservative PM Harold Macmillan. Winston Churchill, who could certainly have been a Duke, an Earl, or anything else, always refused to accept anything more than a knighthood, not wanting to leave his beloved House of Commons.

Finally there are the 379 Life Peers, men and women of distinction in politics and other fields, awarded a lifetime-only peerage by the Government. They include the Judicial Life Peers, or Law Lords.

The House of Lords is the supreme judicial authority for England and Wales, serving as the ultimate Court of Appeal under the Lord Chancellor. The Lord Chancellor also acts as leader of the House of Lords, fulfilling much the role of the Speaker in the Commons, but with fewer powers.

Incidentally, if you're watching proceedings in the House of Lords on television, and notice some old gent laying his head back on his seat and closing his eyes – he's not *necessarily* having a quiet kip. Most members of the Lords are getting on and deafness is a common problem. To help the old boys out, they've installed little round loudspeakers in the backs of the chairs – so that apparently-dossing peer might simply be concentrating hard on the debate. That's the official story anyway ... They have the same sort of loudspeakers in the Commons, so maybe they're not really nodding off either.

WHO NEEDS LORDS?

The very existence of the House of Lords still comes under fire from our more radically-minded people. Reform the place, they cry. Better still, abolish it altogether!

But the House of Lords still has its uses, particularly when the Government has a vast majority and so everything passes through the House of Commons very easily.

It gives retired Ministers and other politicians a place to go, somewhere where they can still make the odd speech and feel they're still taking part in national affairs. Through the system of Life Peers it allows distinguished people, including non-politicians, to make their contribution.

It also reassures the once-ruling aristocratic families that they aren't entirely forgotten. They can still have a voice, even if a limited one, in the affairs of the nation.

FADING POWERS

Once the Lords, under the king, ruled the country. For a long time the House of Lords ruled the country by virtually controlling the

House of Commons. Now all those old powers have been stripped away. The Lords can do no more than delay the decisions of the Commons – and not all of those.

It can ensure that any new measure is thoroughly debated and discussed before it becomes law. It can force the Government of the day to justify its actions in public.

Nor are the Lords automatically easier on a Conservative government – just the opposite. The Lords know they're quite safe when the Conservatives are in – which means they feel free to kick up more trouble. If they give a Labour government too hard a time, some of those more radical members just might start thinking about abolition again . . .

There's an old saying, 'every Englishman loves a Lord'. They still do. The House of Lords is a typically British institution. Amazingly enough, it works. And as they say in the USA, 'If it ain't broke, don't fix it!'

GOVERNMENT BY THE COMMONS

But although the House of Lords has its place, the country is governed by the democratically elected House of Commons. There are 650 members of Parliament in all, 523 from England, 38 from Wales, 72 from Scotland, 17 from Northern Ireland.

THE PARTY OF GOVERNMENT

The political party which gets a clear majority in the House of Commons in a general election becomes the party of government – however small that majority may be. If no one party gets an overall majority this is known as a hung Parliament. You can be the party of government with a majority of one – but to make things work reasonably well, a majority of at least three or four is needed. You

can't have the government falling because someone gets a cold or gets stuck in traffic.

Politics can be a pretty ruthless business. In times of crisis when a government has a critically small majority, ailing MPs are hauled out of hospital and carried in to vote on stretchers. It's important for the government to win every vote. If the government is defeated on a major issue (called a motion of confidence) it's supposed to resign and call another election.

THE WHIPS

To make sure all party members, government or opposition, turn up to vote for their respective parties, they are organised by a group of officials, somewhat sinisterly known as the 'Whips'. In the hunting field, the job of the whippers-in is to keep a potentially unruly pack of hounds in order – which shows what governments think of their back-bench MPs.

Both government and opposition have their own Whips' Offices. The Whips issue printed instructions which are underlined in order of urgency. A one-line whip means that an MP's attendance at a particular debate is 'requested'. Two lines means MPs 'should' attend. A three-line whip means 'Be there or else!' Illness is no excuse – being dead is probably only just good enough.

THE WHIPS GET TOUGH

Recently there have been accusations that the Government Whips have been using harsh methods to bring Tory MPs into line. Affairs in Europe have provoked a number of Tories to threaten rebellion. There have been stories of potential rebels emerging white-faced and trembling from a going-over by the Whips . . . tales of people being told that if they vote the wrong way they can say goodbye forever to any kind of career in Government. The

ON A THREE LINE WHIP, EVERYBODY HAS TO TURN UP TO VOTE

"IT'S AN AYE, HE NODDED HIS HEAD"
"NO IT SHOOK I TELL YOU!"

Whips, of course, deny all these rumours, saying it's all done by kindness – but then, they would, wouldn't they?

You may wonder who on earth would want to be a Whip, but a job in the Whips' Office is often the first step toward Parliamentary promotion – witness a certain John Major.

A PERFECT PAIR

To make life a bit easier, MPs are sometimes allowed to 'pair'. This isn't some peculiar form of Parliamentary mating. It simply means that an MP from the Government side makes an agreement with one from the Opposition. They'll both be absent from the vote at the same time – so the Government majority isn't affected. When there's a three-line whip, no pairing is allowed.

CALL ME MADAM

The most important single official in the House of Commons is the Speaker – who doesn't actually speak. (At least, only when ticking off the House for its frequently rowdy behaviour with a stern cry of 'Order! Order!')

Nevertheless, the Speaker holds an extremely powerful position, enforcing the rules and calling upon members to speak. So he, or she, has to know everyone's face – and their name and constituency too!

At the time of writing, the Speaker of the House is actually a she. The popular Mrs Betty Boothroyd is the House's first woman speaker.

(One radical MP was heard to mutter that if they were going to keep up these antiquated customs they might just as well get someone who looks good in robes and black stockings.)

NAMING THE GUILTY

The Speaker is elected by the MPs themselves, and is honour bound not to show favour to either party. He, or in this case she, is an extremely powerful and influential official, with considerable powers of discipline.

Occasionally a Member of Parliament will break the rules of the House. This could mean rowdy behaviour, constantly interrupting another speaker, or even 'unparliamentary language'. (In practice this last seems to mean using direct insult – indirect insult seems to be okay. For instance, you're not allowed to call someone a liar – but you can indicate, as Winston Churchill once did, that a fellow member is guilty of 'terminological inexactitude'.)

If an MP persists in offending, the Speaker can order him or her to leave the Chamber for the rest of the session. If they refuse the

Speaker can 'name' them. She will say, 'I name Whoever for disregarding the authority of the Chair.'

The Leader of the House, the MP who is the senior Government spokesman, will then move that the MP be 'suspended from the service of the House' – in other words, expelled for a set number of days. (Like being sent home from school.)

THE RELUCTANT SPEAKER

Incidentally, it's customary for the Speaker, once elected, to put up a sort of mock struggle and have to be dragged to the Speaker's Chair by two other MPs – one of whom must be the longest-serving MP, the Father of the House.

This goes back to the days when the Chair was a political hot seat. You might find yourself forced to defend the Commons against the king – a dangerous business.

A KING DEFIED

This happened in 1642 when Charles I entered the House of Commons with an armed escort – something no monarch has ever done before or since – determined to arrest five MPs who had defied his authority.

The Speaker, Mr Lenthall, defied the king, refusing to say where the wanted MPs, who'd all cleared off, could be found. *'May it please Your Majesty, I have neither eyes to see, nor tongue to speak in this place, but as the House is pleased to direct me, whose servant I am here.'*

Mr Lenthall's memory has been revered ever since – and since then no monarch has been allowed even to enter the House of Commons. That's why the Queen's Speech, on the Opening of

Parliament, is delivered to both Lords and Commons crammed into the House of Lords for the occasion.

COALITIONS AND ALLIANCES

If a party can't get the majority it needs it can still govern by forming an alliance with one of the smaller groups in Parliament. (This used to mean the Irish MPs – today it's more likely to be the Liberal Democrats.)

In times of national emergency – like an extreme economic crisis or, more usually, a war – a coalition government may be formed, with the Cabinet picked from leading members of both parties (like the World War II Cabinet, with the Conservative leader Churchill as Prime Minister, Labour leader Attlee as Deputy PM, and MPs from both parties in the War Cabinet).

CABINET CONTROL

Largely for practical and administrative reasons, the power of Parliament has been more and more concentrated in the Cabinet – the inner group of important Ministers led by the Prime Minister. (Everyone in the Cabinet is a Minister, but not every Minister is in the Cabinet.)

In a Conservative government members of the Cabinet are appointed by the PM. In a Labour administration, the members of the Cabinet are voted in by their fellow MPs.

ALL TOGETHER NOW

The accepted idea is that the Cabinet governs by 'consensus'. The Prime Minister consults with his (or her) colleagues and a generally agreed common policy is hammered out. Members of the Cabinet may argue amongst themselves, but they're supposed to present a common front to Parliament and to the rest of the country. This is called the principle of Cabinet solidarity – a principle much strained in Maggie Thatcher's day.

PAPERS – WHITE AND GREEN

The future plans of the government are often spelled out in what are called 'white' and 'green' papers.

Green papers say what the government is thinking about doing. White ones, which are more detailed, describe what they've decided to do.

Sometimes the papers are simply used for discussion in Cabinet. However, if the government is planning some major reform, both green and white papers will be published, so they can be debated in Parliament as a whole.

They will also be published in the press so the whole country gets a chance to know what the government is thinking.

THE PM

The post of Prime Minister is extremely powerful, particularly in a Conservative government. For a start, a Conservative PM gets to *pick* the Cabinet, handing out all the top jobs. What's more the PM can 're-shuffle' at will, not only changing the jobs round but sacking some ministers and appointing others. (Awkward ministers can find themselves out in the cold – or worse still, sent off to sort out Northern Ireland.) Sometimes a strong-minded Prime Minister can virtually hijack the Cabinet, behaving like an American or European President. (See Maggie Thatcher, earlier.) However, this can be dangerous. In time an oppressed and bullied Cabinet may summon the courage to oust the PM. (See Maggie Thatcher – again!)

THE RANK AND FILE

Most members of the House of Commons never get to climb to the top of what Disraeli called the greasy pole and become Prime Minister – or even reach Cabinet rank.

They're called backbenchers – because they sit on the benches to the rear of the debating chamber. The front bench is reserved for PM and Cabinet. But most backbenchers nurse a burning hope that one day they'll be moving forwards – if some of those old ones at the front will only be good enough to resign or die off . . .

WHAT'S IT WORTH?

In the bad old days MPs didn't get paid at all. If you didn't have a private income, you obviously weren't worthy. Eventually salaries were introduced, though they stayed low for a very long time. It was still much much easier to be an MP if you were well-heeled. There were ways round this, of course. Generally speaking wealthy businessmen supported the Conservative cause while Labour was helped out by trade unions.

HIGHER AND HIGHER!

Over the years, MPs' salaries have risen steadily. In January 1991, MPs' salaries went up to £28,970 a year. Their salaries are now linked to a senior grade in the Civil Service. The Cabinet does even better, with salaries ranging from £48,381 a year to as high as £59,914 in 1991.

At the very top, the PM pulls down a whopping £72,533. Then again, perhaps it's not all that much for running the whole country. Top salaries in industry are higher by far. (The leader of the House of Lords, the Lord Chancellor, got £91,500 in 1991 – far more than the PM.)

MAKING ALLOWANCES

As well as his salary, an MP gets almost as much again in secretarial and research allowances. Most MPs employ research assistants. A surprising, or maybe not so surprising, number of them are attractive young women, often from America. (Eyebrows were raised not so long ago at the employment of a Miss Pamella Bordes, who was thought to have some distinctly extra-Parliamentary talents.)

If an MP's home is outside London he gets a living-in-London allowance of about £1000 a month. (All MPs must have accommodation within a mile of Westminster.) There's also a car allowance, an index-linked pension of over 50 per cent of salary and a tax-free severance allowance of one year's salary on retirement.

MOONLIGHTING MPs

And that's not all. MPs (mostly Conservatives but some Labour ones too) often pick up lucrative part-time jobs on the board of various businesses. Others become highly-paid 'consultants' to some industry or special interest group. It's all quite above board – as long as the MP records the fact on the Parliamentary Register. MPs are supposed to make *all* their commercial connections public – it's called 'declaring an interest'.

NICE LITTLE EARNERS

These rules have to be taken very seriously. Back in the seventies, Reggie Maudling, a Conservative Home Secretary, was accused of having his business interests far too closely linked with those of a dodgy entrepreneur called Poulson.

Reggie Maulding had never been entirely trusted by his fellow Tories. Tubby, laid-back and brilliant, he was a sort of Billy Bunter of politics. He seemed to do well without trying and was often accused of being lazy. He was also suspected of that most damning quality of all for a Tory MP – that of being 'too clever by half'. When Poulson and his business associates came under investigation, Maudling was forced to resign. Since the Home Secretary is in charge of the police, he'd have been investigating himself!

REGGIE'S DOWNFALL

In 1977, Poulson, Reggie Maudling, another Conservative MP called Coddle, and a Labour backbencher called Roberts were all summoned before a special Select Committee. All three politicians were accused of involvement in Poulson's dodgy dealings, and all three were censured by the committee. (In true politician style, all three promptly claimed they'd been exonerated.)

There was talk of expelling Maudling and the others from Parliament, but in the end no action was taken. Nevertheless, their political careers, especially poor Reggie's, were virtually over.

TRAVEL AND TALKING

There are also speaking fees to be earned. As much as £1000 can be earned by making an after-dinner speech, with really top-

PRIVATE MEMBER'S BILL

ranking MPs earning several times as much. (Even today, at something like £20,000 a speech, Maggie Thatcher doesn't come cheap.)

Other, and strictly legitimate, perks for MPs include unending offers of hospitality and the chance of lots of free trips, both in Britain and abroad. It's amazing how many MPs go on fact-finding missions, or attend conferences, in places like the Bahamas and the South of France . . .

IN THE BEGINNING

So how do you get to be an MP and enjoy all this lovely loot? Many aspiring MPs start off by being active in local politics. Some may have been local councillors.

Labour candidates will most probably have been proposed by a trade union or selected by a local constituency association.

The Tories have a more centralised system than the Labour Party. Conservative candidates first have to be passed as suitable by the party's Parliamentary Selection Board.

Whatever his or her party, the would-be MP will have to be selected as a candidate by a local constituency association. There are invariably a number of candidates to be *the* candidate. The constituency association will give them all a good grilling. Such associations often interview wives or husbands as well before making up their minds.

Most of the candidates selected will be white and male, and they'll probably be middle class as well – even in the Labour Party. There are more women in Parliament than there used to be, but it's still twice as tough for a woman to pass the selection committee. Members of ethnic groups find it even tougher. These days some local Labour parties practise positive discrimination in favour both of women and of ethnic minorities. But there's still a long way to go. In 1991 for instance there were 44 women MPs, one Asian and one black MP and things haven't changed much since.

INTO THE FRAY

Once selected the lucky candidate must wait for the chance to fight an election. It could be a by-election caused by the death or retirement of some individual MP. More likely the candidate will have to wait till the next general election.

To make things even tougher, the safe seats are naturally reserved for established MPs. New candidates will usually only be chosen for the impossible-to-win seats. This explains why, at election time, Young Conservative chinless wonders can be seen trying to convince the unemployed workers of Liverpool of the virtues of Toryism. It also explains the presence of that stalwart trade unionist, preaching socialism to the shocked old ladies of Eastbourne. Such candidates aren't expected to win. They're just practising – being given a chance to show their mettle, and to be hardened in the election battle.

SUCCESS AT LAST

The candidate who is tough and determined enough to survive may one day be allowed to stand for a slightly less hopeless seat – and may actually win it. (Sometimes new MPs may be swept in by a landslide, winning seats no-one really thought they could win. Lots of Labour candidates were amazed to find themselves MPs in 1945.)

Victorious at last, the successful candidate goes up to Westminster – and finds the place bulging at the seams. The proud new MP spends weeks fighting for a cubby-hole containing a desk and a telephone. What sort of a work-place is this anyway, the new arrival might well wonder? And where are the loos?)

MAIDEN SPEECH

Sooner or later the new MP has to face the ordeal of making his or her maiden speech. In theory this shouldn't prove too painful. The Parliamentary convention is that maiden speeches should be bland and non-controversial, and be received with polite applause. The convention isn't always observed.

THE MAIDEN SPEECH
"THE HUMAN BRAIN STARTS WORKING THE MOMENT YOU ARE BORN,
AND NEVER STOPS UNTIL YOU STAND UP TO SPEAK IN PUBLIC"

JESSEL

In 1935 a writer/MP called A P Herbert used his maiden speech to introduce a new Divorce Bill. *'That speech was no maiden,'* observed Winston Churchill afterwards. *'It was a brazen hussy!'* And it's no surprise to hear that when Margaret Hilda Thatcher finally got into Parliament in 1959, she started her Parliamentary career with an exceptional maiden speech. For a new MP Maggie was amazingly lucky. She'd scarcely got her feet inside Parliament when she came second in the ballot for time to introduce a Private Member's Bill. (More about this system later.)

So Maggie's maiden speech wasn't the usual string of clichés. Instead it was the introduction to her own pet measure, The Public Bodies (Admission to Meetings) Act – a new law to give the Press a right of access to council meetings. Apparently Maggie spoke for 27 minutes without notes, delivering a crisp, concise speech loaded with statistics. Everyone was impressed. Barbara Castle, the Labour MP, said she would support the Bill even if her party opposed it. Henry Brooke, then Minister of Housing, was filled with admiration. *'No words of mine can be too high praise for the brilliance with which the member for Finchley opened the debate.'* Maggie was on her way. (Unusually for a Private Member's Bill, Maggie's Act made it right through the Parliamentary process, becoming law in 1960.)

THE PARLIAMENTARY PALACE

The buildings making up the two Houses of Parliament are formally known as the Palace of Westminster. The present-day Palace covers 8 acres of ground. There are over 11,000 rooms, 100 staircases and 35 lifts.

The heart of Westminster is the Central Lobby with its high vaulted roof and huge brass chandelier. The Lobby, the meeting place of Parliament, stands between Lords and Commons. To the north, corridors lead to the House of Commons Lobby and

Chamber, to the south to the House of Lords.

Beyond the Commons is the famous clock tower, housing Big Ben. (Properly speaking Big Ben doesn't mean the actual clock, but the bell which sounds the hours. It came into use in 1859.)

But to most people Parliament means the two debating chambers, Lords and Commons, now familiar to us all since Parliament began to be televised.

THE DOOR TO THE COMMONS

SINCE CHARLES I TIME NO MONARCH HAS BEEN ALLOWED PAST THIS DOOR — WITH THE EXCEPTION OF GEORGE V WHO WAS ALLOWED TO INSPECT BOMB DAMAGE WHEN THE HOUSE RECEIVED A DIRECT HIT IN 1942

BLACK ROD
EVERY YEAR, AT THE OPENING OF PARLIAMENT, BLACK ROD, THE MESSENGER FROM THE LORDS, GOES TO SUMMON THE COMMONS INTO THE PRESENCE OF THE QUEEN AND HER PEERS. THE DOOR OF THE COMMONS SLAMMED SHUT IN HIS FACE IN A RITUAL DATING BACK TO THE TIME WHEN CHARLES I TRIED TO ARREST 5 MP.S. BLACK ROD HAS TO KNOCK POLITELY AND ASK PERMISSION TO ENTER — THE COMMONS HAS SHOWN WHO'S BOSS!

CHURCHILL HAD THE DOORWAY REBUILT FROM THE ORIGINAL PIECES — THE BOMB SCARS ARE STILL THERE.

"POLITICS IS ALMOST AS EXCITING AS WAR, AND EVERY BIT AS DANGEROUS, ALTHOUGH IN WAR YOU CAN ONLY BE KILLED ONCE — IN POLITICS MANY TIMES!" CHURCHILL

STATUES OF CHURCHILL AND LLOYD GEORGE, TWO OF PARLIAMENTS GREATEST ORATORS. MP.S REGULARLY RUB THE STATUES' FEET FOR LUCK WHEN ABOUT TO GIVE A DIFFICULT SPEECH — THE FEET HAVE BEEN RUBBED SMOOTH WITH THE ATTENTION.

DOORKEEPER'S CUBICLE IN THE ARM OF THE SEAT IS A CONCEALED DRAWER CONTAINING SNUFF FOR THE USE OF MP.S

THE INNER MAN – AND WOMAN

Until 1773 there wasn't a bite or a sup to be had in the House. MPs used to bring in their own supplies, and sit in the Chamber munching pies and sucking oranges. Today there are nine bars (all that talking makes you thirsty), four restaurants, four cafeterias and a Members' Tea Room.

CATERING FOR ALL TASTES

THEIR LORDS AND LADYSHIPS' HOUSE

At the southern end of the Lords Chamber is the Throne, from which the Queen reads her speech at the opening of Parliament. (When the Lords is actually in session, privileged peers can sit on the steps.)

In front of the Throne is the famous woolsack, in reality a broad, red-covered seat on which sits the Lord Chancellor, who acts as Speaker of the House of Lords. (The woolsack is actually a red cushion, and it symbolises the days when much of Britain's prosperity came from wool.)

In front is the Table of the House, where the clerks sit. The Mace, a sort of silver club symbolising royal authority, rests on the woolsack behind the Lord Chancellor.

The Lords' benches are upholstered in red leather. They run along both sides of the House, five rows of them, Government benches to the right of the throne, Opposition to the left. (There are cross-benches in front of the woolsack for peers who can't make up their minds – or rather, for those who support no particular party.)

At the other end of the chamber is a formal barrier known as the bar (no, not that kind). There are galleries around three sides of the house. The one at the far end, opposite the throne, is the press gallery, with the broadcasting gallery in its centre.

THE OTHER PLACE

The Commons Chamber is always referred to in the Lords as 'another place'. (To the Commons, of course, the Lords is the 'other place'.) The Commons chamber is laid out on very similar lines to that of the Lords.

The Speaker's Chair stands on steps at the north end. Before it is the Table of the House, where the Clerk of the House sits with his assistants. At the head of the table rests the Mace – the Commons have one as well.

The benches, upholstered this time in green, face each other across the length of the table. The green carpet running down the centre has a red stripe running down either side. The stripes are two swords-length apart – to remind members to settle their differences with words rather than with cold steel.

There were duels in the Chamber in 1779 and in 1780, but these days the Speaker disapproves of that sort of thing. (In the members' cloakroom there are little pegs for MPs to hang up their swords.)

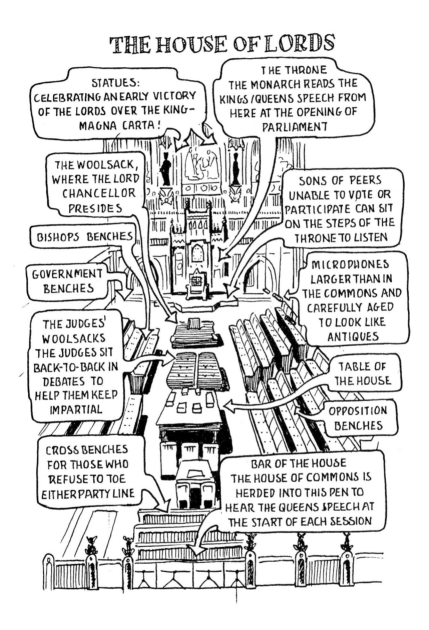

The Government sits on the Speaker's right, the Opposition on his or her left. The nobs – Prime Minister, Cabinet Ministers and so on, sit on the front benches on the Government side. Ordinary MPs, the backbenchers, sit behind them.

On the Opposition front bench sit the Leader of the Opposition and his Shadow Cabinet. They form a sort of mock Government, all hoping one day to change sides in the House and become a real one.

Ministers, and official spokesmen for the Opposition, speak from despatch boxes, which stand on their respective ends of the table. Humbler MPs speak from where they're sitting, bobbing up and down in an attempt to catch the Speaker's eye. At the far end of the room is the bar, a formal barrier as in the Lords.

It's worth mentioning that MPs can't be sued for libel over anything said in the House – they're protected by Parliamentary Privilege. According to the Bill of Rights of 1689: *'Freedom of speech and debates or proceedings in Parliament ought not to be impeached or questioned in any place or court outside Parliament.'*

PLAYING TO THE GALLERY

There are galleries around all four sides of the House. Opposite the Speaker's Chair is the Strangers' Gallery, from which the public can watch the debates. The one above and behind the Speaker's Chair is the Press and Broadcasting Gallery. Parliament has a rather complicated relationship with the broadcasting media.

GENTLEMEN OF THE PRESS

It began, and continues of course, with the Press. There are the Gallery Reporters, who cover debates from the Press Gallery, and the Parliamentary sketch writers who deal with events in a lighter,

THE HOUSE OF COMMONS
FROM THE VISITORS GALLERY

THE COMMONS ORIGINALLY SAT IN THE NARROW ST. STEPHEN'S CHAPEL, WITH
THE SPEAKER'S CHAIR ON THE ALTAR STEPS; HENCE THE PRESENT CHAIR IS ON
A RAISED STEP, TO WHICH MPs BOW WHEN ENTERING, AND HENCE ALSO THE
ARRANGEMENT OF SEATS IN TWO FACING ROWS – AND THE TWO PARTY SYSTEM ?

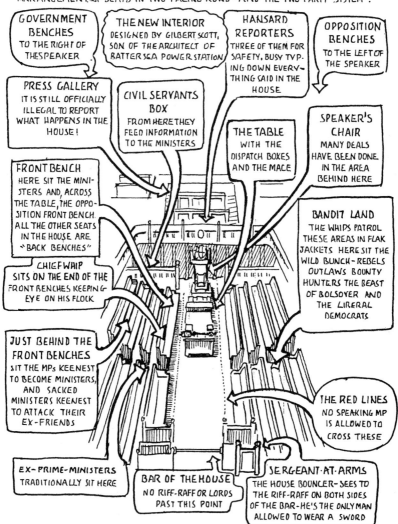

GOVERNMENT BENCHES
TO THE RIGHT OF THE SPEAKER

THE NEW INTERIOR
DESIGNED BY GILBERT SCOTT, SON OF THE ARCHITECT OF BATTERSEA POWER STATION

HANSARD REPORTERS
THREE OF THEM FOR SAFETY. BUSY TYPING DOWN EVERYTHING SAID IN THE HOUSE

OPPOSITION BENCHES
TO THE LEFT OF THE SPEAKER

PRESS GALLERY
IT IS STILL OFFICIALLY ILLEGAL TO REPORT WHAT HAPPENS IN THE HOUSE !

CIVIL SERVANTS BOX
FROM HERE THEY FEED INFORMATION TO THE MINISTERS

THE TABLE
WITH THE DISPATCH BOXES AND THE MACE

SPEAKER'S CHAIR
MANY DEALS HAVE BEEN DONE IN THE AREA BEHIND HERE

FRONT BENCH
HERE SIT THE MINISTERS AND, ACROSS THE TABLE, THE OPPOSITION FRONT BENCH. ALL THE OTHER SEATS IN THE HOUSE ARE "BACK BENCHES"

CHIEF WHIP
SITS ON THE END OF THE FRONT BENCHES KEEPING EYE ON HIS FLOCK

BANDIT LAND
THE WHIPS PATROL THESE AREAS IN FLAK JACKETS HERE SIT THE WILD BUNCH – REBELS OUTLAWS BOUNTY HUNTERS THE BEAST OF BOLSOVER AND THE LIBERAL DEMOCRATS

JUST BEHIND THE FRONT BENCHES
SIT THE MPs KEENEST TO BECOME MINISTERS, AND SACKED MINISTERS KEENEST TO ATTACK THEIR EX-FRIENDS

THE RED LINES
NO SPEAKING MP IS ALLOWED TO CROSS THESE

EX-PRIME-MINISTERS
TRADITIONALLY SIT HERE

BAR OF THE HOUSE
NO RIFF-RAFF OR LORDS PAST THIS POINT

SERGEANT-AT-ARMS
THE HOUSE BOUNCER– SEES TO THE RIFF-RAFF ON BOTH SIDES OF THE BAR– HE'S THE ONLY MAN ALLOWED TO WEAR A SWORD

more entertaining way. Most important of all are the Lobby Correspondents, a privileged group of about 150 journalists who are allowed to talk to members informally in the Members' Lobby outside the Chamber. However, the price they pay for being on the inside is a certain loss of independence. If they are told anything 'on lobby terms' they must keep the source confidential. Similarly, they are given 'non-attributable briefings'. This means they can repeat what they've been told, but mustn't say who told them. Governments use these briefings for kite flying, a sort of controlled leak. If the Government has its doubts about some plan or scheme it can leak the details and get the public's reaction – and still deny everything later if it seems best.

RADIO DAYS

Parliament also had to come to terms with the radio, not without some early doubts. Daily broadcasting of Parliament began in 1978 and is now an accepted feature.

TELEVISION TIMES

Television was received with even more suspicion. Strangely enough the Lords were the most adventurous, allowing television into their Chamber in 1985. The Commons voted to allow the televising of their proceedings in 1988, and regular television broadcasting began in 1989. There were the usual dire predictions that TV would mean the ruin of Parliament. The early days saw a good deal of 'doughnutting'. An MP speaking on camera would find his neighbours' heads appearing over his shoulders, crowding their way into the picture.

Parliament seems to have got used to TV by now and largely ignores it – although we'll see later how at least one ex-Prime Minister thinks television has corrupted Question Time.

STARTING THE DAY

Parliament's working day starts at 2.25 in the afternoon – except on Fridays when it begins at 9.25 am so everyone can get away early for the weekend.

A policeman's long-drawn-out cry of 'Speaker!' rings out and a little procession moves through the central lobby. It consists of the Commons Bar doorkeeper, in knee-breeches, silk stockings and white gloves, followed by the Serjeant-at-Arms carrying the mace. Behind them walks the Speaker, followed by train-bearer, chaplain and secretary. (Male Speakers were elaborately dressed in court suit, black silk robe and train. The current Speaker, Mrs Betty Boothroyd, presents a simpler, more modern appearance.)

Once the Speaker is installed in the Chamber, the day begins with prayers. Or, as a schoolboy once put it, *'The Chaplain looks at the members of Parliament and prays for the country.'*

WHAT ARE THEY ALL DOING IN THERE?

Part of Parliament's job is to discuss the affairs of the nation. Frequently a debate on some pressing issue will be decided on by the Government or agreed by Government and Opposition. Debates are usually opened by the Minister of the Department most concerned with the issue being discussed, and his opposite number in the Shadow Cabinet. They are wound up by a junior Minister and a junior Opposition spokesman.

SUPPLY AND DEMAND

Sometimes the Opposition gets the chance to choose the topic. The rules of the House of Commons provide for 20 days in each session where the Opposition may choose the subject for debate. Seventeen of these days go to the main opposition party – Labour or Conservative, whichever one's *not* in power. The smaller parties get the other three days.

Originally these days were called 'supply days' because the government's public spending, the money 'supply', was supposed to be the subject under discussion. Over the years the discussion widened to give the Opposition a chance to criticise any and all Government measures, and supply days became Opposition Days.

TIME GENTLEMEN PLEASE

It's impossible to predict exactly how long a major debate will take. Often the Speaker will attempt to speed things up by begging MPs to keep their contributions brief – ten minutes is the usual suggestion.

"ALCOHOL IS A VERY NECESSARY ARTICLE. IT ENABLES PARLIAMENT TO DO THINGS AT 11.00 AT NIGHT THAT NO SANE PERSON WOULD DO AT 11.00 IN THE MORNING."

SHAW

Occasionally MPs will defy the Speaker and 'filibuster'. This usually involves making enormously long speeches, either to wear down the Government, or to attempt to take up so much time that a bill has to be postponed or even abandoned.

POINT OF ORDER!

Something else which can cause delays is the raising of points of order, when an MP wishes to raise a matter concerning the House's rules of debate. Those same rules lay down that an MP wishing to raise a point of order must be 'covered' – i.e. he must be wearing a hat.

To assist MPs in keeping this rule a couple of battered old felt hats are kept in the Chamber. An MP who wishes to raise a point of order must put on one of these hats and wait for the Speaker to call him.

WHERE DID YOU GET THAT HAT?

In a recent controversial debate, so many MPs wanted to raise points of order that the supply of hats couldn't keep up with demand. Some MPs started making themselves paper hats out of their Order Papers. A heated debate then began as to whether a paper hat could be considered a real hat for the purpose of the rule. The Deputy Speaker, who was unlucky enough to be in charge that day, decided that although a paper hat as such might be acceptable, a paper hat made from an Order Paper wasn't. 'Quite right!' said some MPs. 'Rubbish!' said others. 'What's the difference between one kind of paper hat and another?' The Honourable Members spent so much time discussing this important question of Parliamentary procedure – and trying out various styles of paper hat – that the original debate was almost forgotten . . .

CLEAR THE LOBBIES!

However long the debate, and all-night sittings are not unknown, it eventually has to come to a close. At the end of a debate, the Speaker will first call for a vote, to be expressed simply by cries of 'Aye!' or 'No!' After any keenly-fought debate there will always be conflicting cries of both 'Ayes' and 'Noes' together. Then the Speaker calls 'Clear the Lobbies!'

SUMMONED BY BELLS

This means that a formal vote is about to be taken. The vote is known as a division because the House literally divides itself. Loud bells ring in every room of the House, even the smallest ones, and in a selected number of nearby pubs, clubs and restaurants as well, where it is known MPs converge. Any far-flung MPs are expected to drop what they're doing and dash for the lobbies. (You don't have to *listen* to any of the arguments to know how to vote – you just support your own side.)

Whether they start from the bar of the House of Commons or from the bar of the local pub, MPs have just eight minutes to make it into the lobby of their choice. The Ayes, those voting for the motion under discussion, enter the lobby on the Speaker's right. The 'Nos', those against it, go through the one on the left.

LOCK THE DOORS

Eight minutes after the division bells have been rung, the Speaker calls, 'Lock the doors!' The entrance doors to the two lobbies are immediately and very firmly closed by the House officials. Many a

WAR BY OTHER MEANS
HOW THEY'RE KEPT APART - OR NOT

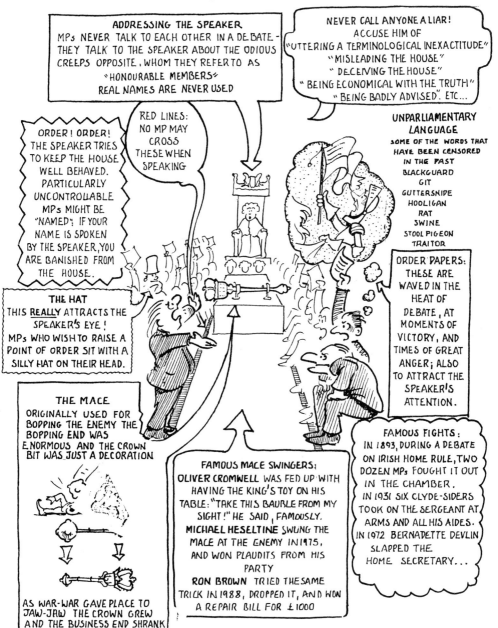

ADDRESSING THE SPEAKER
MPs NEVER TALK TO EACH OTHER IN A DEBATE - THEY TALK TO THE SPEAKER ABOUT THE ODIOUS CREEPS OPPOSITE, WHOM THEY REFER TO AS "HONOURABLE MEMBERS". REAL NAMES ARE NEVER USED

NEVER CALL ANYONE A LIAR!
ACCUSE HIM OF "UTTERING A TERMINOLOGICAL INEXACTITUDE" "MISLEADING THE HOUSE" "DECEIVING THE HOUSE" "BEING ECONOMICAL WITH THE TRUTH" "BEING BADLY ADVISED". ETC...

RED LINES: NO MP MAY CROSS THESE WHEN SPEAKING

UNPARLIAMENTARY LANGUAGE
SOME OF THE WORDS THAT HAVE BEEN CENSORED IN THE PAST
BLACKGUARD
GIT
GUTTERSNIPE
HOOLIGAN
RAT
SWINE
STOOL PIGEON
TRAITOR

ORDER! ORDER!
THE SPEAKER TRIES TO KEEP THE HOUSE WELL BEHAVED. PARTICULARLY UNCONTROLLABLE MPs MIGHT BE "NAMED"; IF YOUR NAME IS SPOKEN BY THE SPEAKER, YOU ARE BANISHED FROM THE HOUSE.

THE HAT
THIS **REALLY** ATTRACTS THE SPEAKER'S EYE! MPs WHO WISH TO RAISE A POINT OF ORDER SIT WITH A SILLY HAT ON THEIR HEAD.

ORDER PAPERS: THESE ARE WAVED IN THE HEAT OF DEBATE, AT MOMENTS OF VICTORY, AND TIMES OF GREAT ANGER; ALSO TO ATTRACT THE SPEAKER'S ATTENTION.

THE MACE
ORIGINALLY USED FOR BOPPING THE ENEMY THE BOPPING END WAS ENORMOUS AND THE CROWN BIT WAS JUST A DECORATION

AS WAR-WAR GAVE PLACE TO JAW-JAW THE CROWN GREW AND THE BUSINESS END SHRANK

FAMOUS MACE SWINGERS:
OLIVER CROMWELL WAS FED UP WITH HAVING THE KING'S TOY ON HIS TABLE: "TAKE THIS BAUBLE FROM MY SIGHT!" HE SAID, FAMOUSLY.
MICHAEL HESELTINE SWUNG THE MACE AT THE ENEMY IN 1975, AND WON PLAUDITS FROM HIS PARTY
RON BROWN TRIED THE SAME TRICK IN 1988, DROPPED IT, AND WON A REPAIR BILL FOR £1000

FAMOUS FIGHTS:
IN 1893, DURING A DEBATE ON IRISH HOME RULE, TWO DOZEN MPs FOUGHT IT OUT IN THE CHAMBER.
IN 1931 SIX CLYDE-SIDERS TOOK ON THE SERGEANT AT ARMS AND ALL HIS AIDES.
IN 1972 BERNADETTE DEVLIN SLAPPED THE HOME SECRETARY...

late-arriving MP has been in grave danger of being squashed.

Once the doors are shut no-one else can get in – and no-one can get out except by going through the door at the other end of the long room. There he passes between two Tellers, one from each party, who tick off his name and register his vote. To prevent impersonation every MP is supposed to hold his head high and say his name in a loud, clear voice.

With the MPs back in the Chamber, the Tellers provide the Speaker with the final voting figures. The Speaker announces that 'the Ayes' (or the Nos) have it!' Inevitably – or almost inevitably – the Government wins – and the main debate is over. Everyone dashes from the Chamber. Well, not quite everyone . . .

NOW THE TECHNOLOGICAL REVOLUTION GIVES PARLIAMENT THE
CHANCE TO UPDATE ITS VOTING SYSTEM

ADJOURNMENT DEBATES

One junior Minister and one MP remain, and another curious Parliamentary ritual takes place.

By applying in advance, and taking his chance in a ballot, a backbench MP can be awarded an adjournment debate. This gives him the right to raise an issue of his choice in a 15-minute speech, *in the presence of a Minister*. A Minister, however junior, must be present during the speech. What's more he must deliver a proper, considered reply, in a speech of about the same length.

Adjournment debates usually take place at the end of the session, sometimes in the small hours of the morning. Very often the only ones present are the Speaker, the Minister, and the MP, a lonely trio surrounded by acres of empty green benches.

Nevertheless, however small, or even non-existent his audience, the backbench MP has had his say. He has made his speech and obtained his Ministerial reply, and his topic has been publicly aired.

It will be covered in Hansard, the journal that reports all the proceedings of Parliament. It may even be picked up and reported in the local paper . . .

LAYING DOWN THE LAW

The main business of Government is to make, or change, the law of the country. A draft law is called a Bill. It goes through several stages, all of which mean a lot of work for Parliament.

FIRST READING

The Bill is presented to the House of Commons by the appropriate Minister. This stage is really a formality – the name of the Bill is simply read out.

SECOND READING

This time the Bill gets talked about. The Government supports and defends it, the Opposition will probably try to tear it to bits. Changes may be suggested and eventually there's a vote. Since the Government, by definition, has a majority, the Bill will usually pass its second reading.

Not always, though. On a really controversial Bill – like the ones concerning the Maastricht treaty, or the threatened closure of a number of coalmines, rebellious backbenchers may threaten to vote against their own Government.

It's the job of the Whips to assess the mood of the backbench MPs – and to bring any potential rebels back into line.

COMMITTEE STAGE

Past the hurdle of the second reading, the Bill is sent before a Standing Committee. (It's the Committee that stands, the members can sit down.)

A Standing Committee consists of anything from 16 to 50 members, drawn from all parties, though it always includes a Government Minister.

Bills can be, and usually are, long and complicated with many different sections. The Standing Committeee discusses each section in detail, amending and clarifying the Bill if necessary.

REPORT STAGE

When the Committee is reasonably happy with the Bill it goes on to Report Stage, where it is considered by the House in its new form. This time not the Bill itself, but only the amendments, can be discussed.

THIRD READING

The Bill is then discussed in its final form. No great changes can be made this time and the third reading is usually short. The Bill then goes to the Lords.

IN THE LORDS

Procedure in the Lords is largely the same, except that there's no Standing Committee. The Lords can, if they wish, amend the Bill and send it back. The Commons may accept the changes, or they may not. If they reject them the Bill goes to yet another committee to discuss the disputed changes. Once agreement is reached, the Lords pass the Bill.

If agreement can't be reached, and the Lords refuse to pass the Bill, it is said to have 'failed'. Once that would have meant the end of it – but these days it doesn't actually make too much difference. After a year's delay, the Bill goes forward, even without the Lords' consent.

As we've seen earlier, the Lords aren't allowed to interfere with 'Money Bills' at all. Bills dealing with taxation or Government expenditure become law within one month, whether the Lords agree or not.

ROYAL ASSENT

Once it has passed all three stages in both Houses, the Bill is sent for the queen's OK, otherwise known as the Royal Assent. This is really just another formality. Royal Assent hasn't been refused since 1701.

Once a Bill has passed all its stages it becomes an Act of Parliament – and the law of the land.

LORDS TO COMMONS

Sometimes a Bill starts in the Lords and then has to go through the Commons. In this case, pretty much the same procedure takes place – only backwards, so to speak.

THRASHING IT OUT

The point of all this complicated carry-on is that every Bill is well and truly discussed and debated. Before it becomes law a Bill is thoroughly thrashed out, in both Houses and in various commit-tees. Everyone should get a chance to have their say, even if the Government does usually get its way in the end.

JUST MY BILL

As well as the official Government bill there's the Little Orphan Annie of bills, the Private Member's Bill.

These are introduced by backbenchers, who can come from either side of the house, and have won the chance to introduce a Bill in a sort of Parliamentary raffle called a ballot. There are 20 winning tickets, but only about the first six have any real chance of actually becoming law.

ANY SUGGESTIONS?

Private Member's Bills usually concern something close to the member's heart – but any lucky winner who hasn't got a pet project of his own will get plenty of suggestions. An MP who won a place and wasn't sure what to do with it got over 50 suggestions from his hopeful colleagues . . .

Because of the sheer pressure on Parliamentary time such Bills have a high failure rate and don't often become law. However, some very useful Private Member's Bills have made it all the way, like the Domestic Violence Bill of 1976.

TEN MINUTES PLEASE!

Even more of a Parliamentary long-shot are the Ten Minute Bills. To get a chance at one of these the MP must book three weeks in advance, often staying up all night to be first in the queue. Ten

Minute Bills are debated, one each day, on every Tuesday and Wednesday after the seventh week of each Parliamentary session. The proposer has the right to make a ten-minute speech recommending the Bill. If the House accepts the Bill, the proposer walks from the bar of the House to the Table, bowing three times. Such bills seldom make it into law, but they give their subject a useful airing – and the MP proposing them a chance to shine.

BRIGHT AND EARLY

Another cunning backbencher's device is to put down an EDM or Early Day Motion on some topic which the MP hopes will be debated 'at an early day', i.e. sometime in the near future. The chances of this happening are pretty negligible, as the MP well knows – but the very fact of getting it down on the order paper, the Parliamentary agenda of business, means that the topic has been raised . . .

KEEP IT PRIVATE

Private bills usually affect the interests of large groups like public companies, local authorities or British Rail. (Some however concern very personal and individual cases – like a special bill allowing a step-father and daughter to marry.) Private bills are usually, though not invariably, unopposed, and Parliament puts through about 50 a year.

ANY QUESTIONS

Another great Parliamentary institution, very popular with MPs – and their television viewers – is Prime Minister's Question Time.

This takes place every Tuesday and Thursday between 3.15 pm and 3.30 pm.

MPs have to send in their main questions two weeks in advance, so the PM knows at least something about what's coming. He knows he'll find himself facing questions like: 'Is the Prime Minister aware that most people think that he, and the crew of buffoons he calls a Cabinet, couldn't run the average whelk-stall between them?' (Not those exact words, but that's usually the thought.) Either that or he will simply be asked 'to list his engagements for the day'.

The point of this is that after this question has been answered MPs are allowed, if called by the Speaker, to ask *any* question on *any* subject. The idea is to slip in a real killer question as one of these supplementaries. Since he doesn't know the supplementary questions in advance, the PM will find it much harder to be prepared with a snappy answer – though it's the job of his advisers to anticipate all possible questions.

The Leader of the Opposition is allowed three supplementaries. Prime Minister's Question Time usually turns into a one-on-one duel between party leaders. Poor Sir Alec Douglas-Home got so flustered by Harold Wilson's badgering that he once declared, *'The Government has done nothing – from now till the present day!'*

PROTECTING THE PM

Nevertheless, the Prime Minister is well protected. He/she will have gone over his/her answers with a team of advisers beforehand, and will arrive ready to overwhelm his/her attackers with facts and statistics.

A useful Government trick is to get some loyal backbencher to bowl him an easy one. The PM may find himself facing helpful questions on the lines of: 'Is the Prime Minister aware that we all think he is absolutely wonderful and he and his talented Cabinet are doing a grand job?' (Crawl, crawl!) The Opposition usually greet helpful questions like this with shouts of 'Give him a job!' Even with all these advantages Question Time can be quite an ordeal for the PM. Luckily it's all over in 15 minutes – no extra time!

Recently Prime Minister's Question Time, in its present form at least, has been coming under attack. It's felt that it is being used either for the Opposition to score points, or the Government to pat itself on the back, rather than for any attempt to bring out useful information. One journalist said it should be called 'Wasting Time with the PM' and pointed out that John Major had taken so long avoiding answering his first few questions that a whole string of others never even got asked.

Former Conservative Prime Minister Ted Heath, currently the Father of the House – not the oldest but the longest-serving MP – feels the same way. In his view it's largely the fault of television. Now Parliament is being regularly televised, MPs – and PMs – can't resist playing to the camera.

THE FUTURE OF BROADCASTING PARLIAMENT?

'Since the 1970s, Prime Minister's Questions has been turned into a well-rehearsed theatrical show of buffoonery and "soundbites" for the evening news broadcasts ... For the Prime Minister and Leader of the Opposition to be seen shouting at each other twice a week before two baying teams of backbenchers ... is not conducive to good democracy ... The answer must lie in limiting the questions to fields for which the Prime Minister is held responsible. Supplementary questions must be directly relevant to the initial question.'

There are other Question Times in which mere Cabinet Ministers get tormented, but it's far more fun to see the PM getting grilled. Questions to Ministers can also be submitted, and answered, in writing.

WHERE DID EVERYBODY GO?

The House is usually packed at Prime Minister's Question Time. It's packed too when Parliament is in the throes of some great national crisis, a war, or an economic disaster. (Sounds like most days recently ...)

But at other times ... Watch Parliament on TV on an off day and see how the camera desperately tries to avoid showing you acres of empty green benches. Meanwhile some lonely backbencher drones desperately on about the Orkney Herring Fisheries Bill – to a couple of bored fellow-MPs who are just waiting for their own turn to speak ...

OUTSIDE THE CHAMBER

So what are they all up to? Off on round-the-world trips, lucrative lecture tours – or chasing their beautiful research assistants across the Terrace? Well, some of them probably. Most MPs will be hard at work elsewhere.

No MP is expected to attend every debate all the time. The three-line whip system makes sure everyone appears for the vital votes. At other times, MPs do much of their work outside the chamber. To begin with there are letters to be answered, many of them from constituents about their problems. There may be visitors to be shown round. There is research on some vital issue, perhaps to formulate a question in the House, carried out in the beautiful House of Commons Library.

IN COMMITTEE

Above all, there are committees, endless committees, where much of the real work of the House is done. There are the Standing

COMMITTEES

"A COMMITTEE IS A CUL-DE-SAC DOWN WHICH IDEAS ARE LURED, AND THEN QUIETLY STRANGLED"

"A COMMITTEE - A GROUP OF THE UNWILLING, PICKED FROM THE UNFIT, TO DO THE UNNECESSARY" HARKNESS

"WHEN IT IS NOT NECESSARY TO MAKE A DECISION, IT IS NECESSARY NOT TO MAKE A DECISION" FALKLAND

SELECT COMMITTEE SELECTION PANEL SELECTORS

"COMMITTEES ARE EVENTS WHERE THE MINUTES ARE KEPT, AND THE HOURS ARE LOST" GOURD

"A COMMITTEE IS TWELVE MEN DOING THE WORK OF ONE" KENNEDY

HARRISON'S LAW -"FOR EVERY ACTION, THERE IS AN EQUAL AND OPPOSITE CRITICISM"

Committees, scrutinising the Bills already going through Parliament. There are Select Committees, set up to examine some particular aspect of public policy. There are Select Committees on Agriculture, Defence, Education, Arts, Science, Employment, Energy, Environment, Health, Trade and Industry, Social Security, Transport, and Treasury. There are committees on Home Affairs, Foreign Affairs, Welsh Affairs, Scottish Affairs, and Public Accounts. There is even a Committee of Selection, which chooses people to sit on all the other committees.

The old hands tend to dodge all these committees when they can, but the young and keen get grabbed as soon as they arrive. A reluctant English MP found himself drafted on to the Scottish Affairs Committee. He turned up in full highland dress, kilt, sporran, the lot. This annoyed the Scots on the committee so much they chucked him off – which was exactly what he wanted.

HOURS OF WORK

So how – and when – does all this endless work get done? One of the oddest things about Parliament is the way it organises its working time.

Parliamentary life is divided into sessions, each one lasting roughly a year. Sessions are divided into four. The first part usually runs from November till Christmas – about 35 Parliamentary days. The second is from January to Easter – about 50 days. The third runs from Easter till the end of May – about 30 days. The fourth goes from the beginning of June until late July or early August – about 40–50 days.

The working day is even stranger. 9 till 5 it certainly isn't. The House 'sits' from 2.30 pm to 10 pm on Mondays to Thursdays, though urgent and important debates can go on longer. All-night sittings are not unknown. On Fridays the House sits from 9.30 am to 2.30 pm.

NURSING THE CONSTITUENCY

Friday finishes early so the more far-flung MPs can whizz off to look after their constituencies. An MP's constituency is the place that put him in Parliament, and he'd better not forget it. He will do well to live there, at least some of the time, and he and his wife must make frequent appearances at village fêtes and jumble sales. He'll be expected to hold 'Constituency Surgeries' where he can meet the public, listen to their grumbles – and try to do something about them. (Even in the House, he must be alert for constituency issues. Voters will expect to read reports of such speeches as: 'If this motorway goes ahead, the village green in Little Tittering, in *my constituency*, will be totally ruined!')

THE TRANSFORMATION FROM A POLITICIAN..............TO A STATESMAN

WHY DO IT?

When you consider that many MPs hold down other jobs as well, it's a wonder they survive – not to mention their marriages. Cabinet Ministers and the PM, of course, work even harder. Enormous stamina is needed.

Mrs Thatcher was said to manage on four hours of sleep a night. The rest of the time, one way or another, she was working – a 20-hour day! Or as an earlier politician put it, *'When I am not ill, or in bed, I am in Parliament!'*

Why do people do it? Power? Ambition? Publicity? Or even a selfless desire to serve their country? Who knows? Maybe it's all these things – and the sheer thrill of it as well. Lord Randolph Churchill, Winston Churchill's father, an eminent politician and a life-long Parliamentarian, once said, *'I have tried all forms of excitement, from tip-cat to tiger shooting, all degrees of gambling from beggar-my-neighbour to Monte Carlo, but have found no gambling like politics, and no excitement like a big division in the House of Commons . . .'* So perhaps that's the answer.

Politics is the greatest game – and the greatest gamble – of them all . . .

"A POLITICIAN IS A STATESMAN
WHO APPROACHES
EVERY QUESTION WITH AN
OPEN MOUTH"

ADLAI STEVENSON

INDEX

"MAN WILL OCCASIONALLY STUMBLE OVER THE TRUTH, BUT MOST OF THE TIME HE WILL PICK HIMSELF UP AND CONTINUE ON" CHURCHILL

OTHER BOOKS IN PICCADILLY'S
'INFORMATION WITH HUMOUR' SERIES

THE VERY BLOODY HISTORY OF BRITAIN:
Without the Boring Bits
by John Farman

'. . . includes detailed analysis in a chatty narrative style, full of old jokes,
which make it immensely readable.'
School Librarian

A SUSPICIOUSLY SIMPLE HISTORY OF
SCIENCE AND INVENTION:
Without the Boring Bits
by John Farman

'I found it to be one of the most readable, amusing and informative science
books that has come my way for some time . . . Most highly recommended
for anyone who wants to put some humour into teaching . . .'
Education Review – NUT

EUROPE UNITED
by Terrance Dicks

'The best Eurobook . . . bright and amusing . . . intelligent and great fun.'
Harry Enfield in The Sunday Times

A RIOT OF WRITERS:
A Romp Through English Literature
by Terrance Dicks

The trouble with English Literature is that there's a *lot* of it! This book provides an entertaining, informative and hilarious guide to some of the best writers.

GLOOM, DOOM AND VERY FUNNY MONEY:
Economics for Half-Wits
by Neil Innes

'This is an informative and entertaining guide to the world of economics. If you're still a half-wit after reading this book, you've clearly got a good future working in the City.'
Neil MacKinnon, Chief Economist, Citibank